MW01168787

Copyright © 2023

Version 1.034

BULLIES, NARCISSISTS, LIARS, AND MANIPULATORS

A **SURVIVAL GUIDE** FOR DEALING WITH DIFFICULT, NEGATIVE, AND TOXIC PEOPLE.

SERENA ELLISON

Table of Contents

Get the Worksheet

Hi, Serena here. I'd just like to say thank you for your interest in my work. Also, I've created a little companion worksheet to help with your journey. We'll be referring to this worksheet in Chapter 3. But download it now so you'll be ready.

If you're reading this book on a Kindle or an iPad, you can click the link below. Or, paperback readers can type the link into your iPhone or PC. Thanks! - Serena

www.tiny.cc/bullyguide

Introduction

My first encounter with a bully happened in a typical setting: *elementary school*. There was a student in my class who we'll call Freddy. He was a nice boy, and we got along well. At least, we did until the middle of the school year when, all of a sudden, he started acting differently toward me. At first, it wasn't too serious. He would occasionally pull my hair, put insects in my school bag, and tease me whenever I walked by. But I shrugged off these initial incidents with ease. "He was just a boy being a boy," I supposed. However, as the days went by, things started to get progressively worse...

He began to habitually mock my appearance, my squeaky voice, and criticized me whenever I'd make a class presentation. Sometimes I'd turn my head at lunch to find a spoon full of apple sauce flying my way. And one day, I returned to my locker to find gobs of ice cream shoved through the metal vents. But, for as bad as I got it, the smaller boys in the playground got it worse. Freddie started getting into fights. And some of them went far beyond roughhousing.

His change in behavior confused me then. As a young girl, I couldn't understand why his demeanor had shifted so dramatically. I tried my best to ignore him. But his sniping eventually became unbearable. I tried talking to him about it, but he would just walk away and tell me that I was stupid. It got so bad that I didn't even want to play outside anymore because I feared encountering him and tolerating his wrath. I didn't tell anyone about it because I didn't want to be branded the "school tattletale." I had resigned myself to endure the mean comments, the insects, and the shoving. But one day, he took things too far. He told my two best friends that I hated them, and that I was only friends with them because my mom told me to be. He said that I thought they were ugly and that I secretly despised being around them. My friends believed him and told me that they were no longer my besties. My whole eight-year-old world came tumbling down as they ignored me for weeks. I hid in the bathroom during the lunch break and prayed for the weekend to arrive as fast as possible.

One day, my mother finally realized that something was wrong when she asked me if I was excited about the upcoming birthday sleepover. I told her I wasn't invited and started crying. Then I told my mom everything. I told her about the comments, the shoving, the hair-pulling, and the gossip. I wept as my mom held me in her arms and told me that she was going to take care of it. I begged her not to tell the teacher, but she was adamant. "No one is going to *bully* my little girl and get away with it," she exclaimed. That was the first time I had ever heard that word before. It was at that moment that I realized Freddie was a bully, and I was the target of his scorn.

My mother convinced me that *telling someone* was the right thing to do, and she arranged a meeting with my teacher. I told the teacher everything, and she listened patiently. The next morning, my teacher called my friends into the office to explain that Freddy's behavior was inappropriate and that bullying was wrong.

My friends listened and eventually apologized for believing Freddy. They confessed that he had been bullying them too.

After that meeting, I finally had my friends back, and it felt like I could breathe again. The next morning, after some additional nudging from the teacher, Freddy came up to me and apologized for his behavior. I accepted his apology, but I still remained angry with him, and I couldn't understand why someone would bother to engage in such meaningless and malevolent behavior. The situation confused me. That is, until one day, I met Freddy's parents... But that's a story for the next chapter.

This initial excursion into the world of bullying left an impression on me, and I have returned to the topic many times in the last forty years. The slings and arrows of childhood are not easily forgotten. They shape us in ways we may not realize until much later in life. The taunts, the insults, the dismissals... They leave a scar that stays with us throughout our days.

In my case, these wounds sparked a lifelong interest in human behavior and, more specifically, in the reasons why people feel the need to inflict harm on others. As I made the transition from child to adult, I was quick to note the recurrence of these behaviors— not in the schoolyard anymore, but in other domains like the workplace, the barroom, and the internet.

The bullies of our childhood grow up. But not all of them mature. As we age, their tactics and strategies evolve, as does their degree of malevolence. But our adult bullies do not typically rely on kicks and punches. Instead, their assaults take on a more nuanced form.

- Consider the colleague who assigns the brunt of the work to you, and then swoops in at the last minute to collect all the credit.
- Or the former friend who spreads malicious rumors, tarnishing your reputation.
- Or the mother-in-law who shows up unannounced before bedtime, with cookies and candy in hand for the kids.
- Or the uncle who seems intent on making inappropriate jokes at inappropriate times.

Bullies come in all shapes and sizes. They can show up in the form of a stranger, a friend, a spouse, a lover, or a family member. And though the impetus for their behavior might differ, they all share a common goal: they seek to exert control over a situation by exploiting any perceived power imbalances to satisfy their own needs. While their actions might be more muted than those of a schoolyard bully, their negative influence can be just as pernicious.

We have many labels to describe this indignant lot:

- Narcissists
- Sociopaths
- Psychopaths
- Gaslighters
- Haters
- Liars
- Manipulators
- Backstabbers

- Control Freaks
- Drama Queens

Each label signifies a unique cocktail of depravity. The narcissist cares only for his own feelings and will manipulate others to maintain his inflated ego. The sociopath—devoid of conscience—will lie, cheat, and harm others without feeling a twinge of guilt. The gaslighter is an expert at twisting reality, making his victims doubt their own perceptions and memory. There are many others, and we will be discussing each of these archetypes in detail. We'll enumerate their unique tactics and techniques, and provide you with the strategies you'll need to counter their toxicity.

A *toxin* is defined as:

An antigenic poison that causes disease, even when present at low concentrations in the body.

It doesn't take much exposure to a venomous individual before you start feeling the effect that he or she is having on you. Even a small dose of negativity can infiltrate your emotional wellbeing, setting off a chain reaction that can introduce self-doubt, heightened anxiety, stress, and diminished self-esteem. Continual exposure to bullying behavior will adversely effect your quality of life, your relationships, and even your physical health. Therefore, it's essential to develop the skills needed to identify, neutralize, and minimize our exposure to psychologically toxic people whenever possible.

Perhaps you picked up this book because you're currently dealing with your own bully infestation. Or perhaps someone you love is in the crosshairs of a bully's toxic tactics. Whatever your current situation might be, this book should serve as a guiding light, illuminating the shadowy corners where bullies lurk and thrive. We'll pop the hood of the bully brain and reveal the schematic of the clockwork that powers their manipulative machinations.

Be warned that I'm not a miracle worker. Not all relationships can be salvaged. And not every situation can be improved. But, when armed with the right knowledge and mindset, we can significantly diminish the power that bullies have to impact our lives. Equipped with a better understanding of the bully's *modus operandi*, you will be better situated to navigate through the muck of toxicity that so often pervades our personal and professional spaces, and chart a course toward a more peaceful and harmonious life.

Ch. 1: Why do people become bullies?

In the previous chapter, I recounted the tail of the first bully in my life, a little schoolyard tyrant named Freddy. After our teacher intervened, most of his shenanigans stopped, at least the ones that were levied at me. But, as the months went by, I was still perplexed by the question of why someone would resort to bullying behavior in the first place. During the following school year, I got my answer.

One Friday afternoon, both of Freddy's parents arrived at school to pick him up. His parents were recently divorced, and they both thought it was their day to drive. When they saw each other pulling into the same parking lot, it was as if a powder keg had been ignited. Loud shouting ensued, and bitter accusations filled the air. A couple of teachers walked over to help, but Freddy's parents were going at it like rabid dogs. As they bickered, I glanced over to get a look at Freddy. He was standing quietly on the sidewalk, looking down and not saying a word.

Decades have passed since that chaotic Friday afternoon in front of my old schoolhouse. But I can still feel the waves of sadness flush over me now, just as I did when I was a little girl. I can still see that somber image of Freddy, looking so small and befuddled, standing between two belligerent adults, each with daggers in their eyes. How was a fifth grader supposed to know how to cope with all that?

The Vietnamese Buddhist monk Thich Nhat Hanh once wrote:

When another person makes you suffer, it is because he suffers deeply within himself, and his suffering is spilling over.

These days, whenever I encounter a difficult person, I try to remind myself that I don't know the nature of the obstacles that this person has encountered in life. Instead of reacting with hostility or malice, I try to think of young Freddy—trapped in a world of strife and seeking a way to make his powerful emotions heard.

Not all of our bullies have a similarly bumpy backstory. But each time we encounter one, we should at least try to remain cognizant of the disparate fortunes of man. And make an effort to engender the spirits of compassion and empathy whenever possible.

In this chapter, we'll examine the motivations of people who engage in bullying behavior. We'll also look at the impact that bullying has on our mental health. And we'll explore some of the commonly held misconceptions about bullies and their victims. Hopefully, when armed with a comprehensive understanding of the causes of bullying, we'll be better equipped to devise effective strategies to counter the behavior when we spot it.

What is bullying?

Bullying is not just something that happens to young children at school. The US government's anti-bullying initiative (stopbullying.gov) defines it this way:

Bullying is unwanted, aggressive behavior … that involves a real or perceived power imbalance. The behavior is repeated, or has the potential to be repeated, over time.

Bullies will target people who they feel they have power over. This can be due to the bully possessing (or thinking they possess) greater physicality or intellect than the victim. Or, because the bully believes that he occupies a loftier position in a power hierarchy. For example, a restaurant manager might bully a waitress because he feels it is his right to recklessly wield authority over a subordinate. Or a foreman might harass a construction worker because he perceives his supervisory role as a license to demean and belittle the men working under him.

Beyond the use of physical force, bullies might pursue their goals using a diverse toolbox. Their tactics might include:

- intimidation,
- gossip,
- manipulation,
- belittlement,
- undue criticism,
- public humiliation,
- or, exclusion from social activities.

It's important to note that for an assault to be considered "bullying," it usually must manifest as part of a pattern, often repeated multiple times. A single act of aggression—while still immoral—is typically not considered *bullying*. Additionally, we can usually tell if bullying is going on when the victim herself feels that she does not have any power to stop the bully's actions. Bullies often target people with a recognizable vulnerability that can potentially be exploited. And as a result, this vulnerability might prevent the victim from speaking out and taking action that would stop the bullying from continuing.

Why do people bully?

Looking back on my relationship with Freddy, I can remember achieving resolve on the question of why he was the schoolyard bully. But people are complex beings. Not all of our old experiences so easily map onto our new ones. As I look at the guy on the train platform screaming at everyone in his proximity, I know the motivations for his actions are multifaceted. Knowing Freddy's backstory allowed for some understanding of his situation. But when we encounter a new bully in our daily life, a succinct biography is not so readily available. We may stare at such people and wonder:

- "Why are you the way that you are?"
- "What caused you to be this way?"
- "Why can't you see the harm you're doing to others?"

Obviously, there is no single reason that incites someone to become a bully. Each person is unique, and so are their reasons for bullying. However, there are a few general causes that, at least in part, may prompt someone to engage in bullying behavior. In this section, we'll review some of the most common reasons now.

Reason 1: Stress and trauma

We all experience stress in our lives. For some people, the tendency to bully might arise following exposure to high levels of stress that evolve into a traumatic experience. The interplay of distressing emotions in a wounded person can formulate a dangerous cocktail of coping behaviors. Most people have the wherewithal to seek out proactive means of countering stress. But sometimes, people elect to utilize a less desirable outlet for their pain. Bullying might be a tool to cover up some of their own feelings—to prevent the intrusive and painful emotions of their past from resurfacing.

- Screaming at a barista for messing up your coffee order might help you momentarily forget about the harpy of a mother-in-law that resides with you.
- Gossiping about a next-door neighbor's broken marriage might help to mask the pain of your own troubled relationship.
- Publicly belittling a colleague's idea in a meeting might be a way to divert attention from your own workplace insecurities.

Bullies use such behaviors to temporarily mask the negative emotions that are boiling up from within. Of course, these escapades don't actually solve their problems. But the transient thrill that the incident provokes may be enough to prompt the bully to continue the harassment.

Reason 2: Aggressive behaviors

Some people have a volatile temperament. This can stem from a variety of factors, including a harsh environment where aggression is commonplace, or innate personality traits that dispose the person to lean towards impulsivity and reactiveness. Such individuals might view bullying as a normal way of interacting with others or competing for dominance.

Reason 3: Low self-esteem

When it comes to stress and trauma, the pressure comes from outside forces. But low self-esteem is internal. When we hate ourselves, it can be challenging to celebrate the victories of others. Pointing out their flaws and belittling their achievements might come more naturally.

Female bullies seem to be particularly adept at utilizing self-esteem-crushing ploys to bully their victims. They might exploit a colleague's insecurities and prey on her weaknesses to elevate their own sense of worth. This can manifest as hurtful rumors, social exclusion, or malicious gossip. When such behaviors are allowed to go unchecked, they create a toxic environment. And the psychological impact of these encounters can stay with the victim for years.

Reason 4: The bully has been bullied himself

Research shows that people who have been victims of bullying are twice as likely to go on and bully others. Our bullies can seem so invincible, but this is often just a persona they have created to stop themselves from feeling pain. It can be easy, in the midst of being bullied, to vow never to endure that suffering again—even if that means becoming the bully you hated. Sometimes this is a conscious decision. But more often than not, the bully hasn't given much thought to the transformation. Instead, his mind is merely invoking a *subconscious* defense mechanism—one created to cope with the pain.

Reason 5: Difficult home lives

Our home is supposed to be a safe place. It should be where we feel the most secure, where we receive love and acceptance regardless of what's happening in our lives. Unfortunately, for many people, this is not their reality. A persistent underlying factor in the lives of bullies is a lack of parental attention. Bullies often experience a sense of rejection at home from the people who should be giving them the most love in their lives. This is precisely what led my friend Freddy to become a bully. He had to endure parents who constantly fought, while he couldn't do anything to make it better. He felt completely powerless at home, so he demanded power where he could. Of course, this doesn't excuse his bad behavior, but it does provide us with the rationale.

Reason 6: Peer pressure

This may seem strange to a victim of bullying, but sometimes bullies are just trying to maintain relationships that they value but feel are not secure. Peer pressure is a powerful motivator of negative behavior because to keep those we care about, we feel forced to do things we don't want to do. While it is easy to say that people being coerced into bullying by peer pressure should not include these kinds of people in their lives, it is rarely so easy for them to cut these people out. This may lead otherwise peaceful people to become bullies in their own right, once their toxic relationships have desensitized them to the consequences of their actions.

Reason 7: The perceived benefits

It is a sad reality that sometimes people bully simply because they have realized that it is a means to an end. Some bullies have learned that they get what they want when they bully people. And they genuinely enjoy the fruit of their labor. This is rarely the initial reason for someone to become a bully, but it is a common reason to stay a bully long term.

Reason 8: Psychopathy or Sociopathy

Not all schoolyard bullies suffer from a mental condition. But some do. Bullying behavior may be the result of psychopathy or sociopathy—two personality disorders characterized by a lack of empathy and a disregard for the wellbeing of others. Psychopaths and sociopaths often engage in aggressive or deceitful behavior for which they do not have the capacity to experience remorse. And since they don't feel guilty for their actions, their actions will continue until an intervention takes place. We'll be discussing these conditions in Chapter 3 of this book.

None of the above-described reasons are an excuse for bullying.

Bullying is wrong, and no circumstance or experience gives one person the right to treat another person with such malice. However, when dealing with such a toxic individual, we need to remember that (at some level) they're just a wounded organism. If we take the time to understand the impetus for their motivations, then we will be better equipped to take a stand against their intimidations.

Bullying Tactics

In the previous section, we explored why some people engage in bullying behavior and the far-reaching impact this can have on both the victims of the assault and those around them. We'll continue our discussion by focusing on how we can recognize this behavior and navigate the milieu of toxic personality types in general. Learning to spot the signs of toxicity early will aid in mitigating its harmful effects, perhaps even granting us a window of opportunity in which we might take proactive measures to counter their actions.

Not all bullies wear blue jeans. Their presence may be elusive, blending into the social landscape, often hiding behind a veneer of charm. They're found in schoolyards as well as boardrooms. And their tactics change to conform to the environment they inhabit. Their chameleon-like adaptability can make them difficult to identify. Regardless, their actions often leave a similar wake of stress and discomfort in every domain they lurk in. Recognizing these patterns sometimes requires keen observation and an understanding of bullying in all its forms. Below, we'll describe the main types of bullying as commonly encountered in day-to-day life.

1. Physical Bullying

Physical bullying is usually used by those who are larger and stronger than their victims. This type of bullying involves acts of physical aggression, such as hitting, kicking, or pushing. Unlike verbal and social bullying, physical bullying is more conspicuous, often resulting in clear and immediate signs of harm. Nonetheless, it can still occur under the radar, especially when the bully intimidates the victim into silence.

2. Verbal Bullying

Verbal bullying occurs verbally, of course. Here, the bully uses his words to insult, humiliate, or intimidate the victim. It can be more difficult to detect than physical bullying because bullies who use their words as weapons are often quite careful about *where* and *when* they apply their craft. They might take care to ensure that there are no other people around who might have the power to stop them. It is also more challenging to prove because, unlike physical bullying, it does not leave bruises or cuts that can be used as proof. But verbal bullying must be taken just as seriously as physical bullying, as words can be just as harmful as fists, particularly when it comes to the long-term psychological scars that bullying leaves.

3. Social Bullying

Otherwise known as "emotional bullying" or "relational aggression," *social bullying* involves excluding the victim from social activities, spreading rumors about them, or manipulating the dynamics of their social environment with the goal of damaging the victim's reputation. It is similar to verbal bullying, as words are the tools of the trade. However, instead of attacking the victim directly, social bullies attempt to influence the victim's social circle.

Social bullying is even more difficult to detect than verbal bullying because there might be very little interaction between the bully and the victim themselves. This type of bullying is more common in girls than boys, particularly during the school years. But tactics that inflict reputational damage are often utilized by grown adults, family members, or even business competitors.

4. Cyberbullying

Unfortunately, the internet has introduced a new plight to mankind—the "cyberbully." With increased anonymity and distance from their victim's possible defensive actions, cyberbullies use technology and social media to attack with immunity. Cyberbullying can include anything from posting humiliating images to sending physical threats via social media.

Even someone who simply consistently dislikes all your social media posts can be considered a cyberbully.

Cyberbullies are often relentless and exploitative of the anonymity of the digital space. They say things online that they would never dare say to a person in public. But the technology gives them a sense of invulnerability. And, since cyberbullying can be conducted by anyone with a cellphone, the victim may feel a never-ending onslaught of abuse cast their way, sometimes from multiple people at once.

Bully Types

Now that we've discussed four different *bullying tactics* let's examine a few different *bully types*. These topics might sound similar, but they're actually quite different. When we discuss *bullying types*, we're talking about the personalities or character traits that are commonly observed in bullies who occupy different domains. We're all familiar with the classic "schoolyard bully" trope, and some of us are familiar with the "boardroom bully." In this section, we'll discuss a few other common bully archetypes.

Type 1. The Popular Bully

Whether they're the football team captain, the head cheerleader, or the star employee in the office, the popular bully takes advantage of their social standing to pick on others. At school, college, or work, the popular bully creates an exclusive social circle and then bullies everyone who isn't standing inside of it. They often have a group of peers that follow them around like loyal subjects, fueling their ego and supporting their harmful behaviors. These followers—who might be merely acting out of fear of becoming the bully's next target—create a safety net for the popular bully, normalizing their actions and enabling the cycle of abuse to continue. In this hierarchy, the popular bully reigns supreme, using their social power to control, manipulate, and demean those who they perceive as less worthy. Unfortunately, such bullies are often admired for their leadership abilities and praised by peers and superiors alike. The malevolence of their aggressive behaviors may be overlooked due to the bully's charisma and charm. They may even be celebrated for their assertiveness, and their manipulative tactics might be perceived as "strengths." This can lead to a culture of silence and fear, where the victim may feel isolated and helpless under the bully's shadow.

Type 2. The Social Bully

While the *popular bully* is often motivated by a sense of entitlement, the social bully is driven by a desire to control the dynamics of every social situation, perhaps as a way to alleviate their own personal insecurities. This type of bully operates in social groups where Machiavellian tactics (such as rumor, social exclusion, or manipulation) can be readily employed. A social bully might avoid using overtly aggressive tactics, instead electing to damage their victim via pernicious ploys—such as gossip, flirtation, or the twisting of the existing friendship ties. Social bullies maintain their influence in the group by sowing the seeds of discord and managing the social hierarchy that determines "who's in" and "who's out." Such actions can result in deep emotional scars for the victims, causing them to feel rejected and isolated.

Type 3. The Bully-Victim

As we discussed earlier, many bullies become bullies because they were bullied first. What is important to know about these bullies is that they are trying to recapture a lost sense of power. Who they bully rarely has anything to do with the victim other than they are perceived to be weaker than the bully. In some ways, the bully-victim is the easiest to empathize with. Because they have experienced significant pain and are often stuck at the lower ends of the social ladder, it is easier to understand the reasons behind their actions.

Type 4. The Indifferent Bully

The indifferent bully is typically characterized by a lack of empathy or an inability to manifest a proper emotional response following their behaviors. They might be a sociopath, unaware or unconcerned about the damage that their actions may cause. And they might view bullying as just a normal (or entertaining) part of life. Unlike other types of bullies—who may be driven by insecurity or a need to climb the social ladder—the indifferent bully may not have a reason for their aggression. This can make them particularly dangerous, as they do not feel any remorse or guilt—emotions that would otherwise deter a normal person from re-committing such malevolent actions.

Type 5. The Bully Gang

Sometimes, when people are in a group, they act in a way that they wouldn't normally behave if they were alone. In such a scenario (much favored by the writers of Hollywood teen films), a bully gang comes together to intimidate, harass, or belittle their prey. Their collective actions can be extremely damaging, as the victim might feel outnumbered and overwhelmed. The actions of the bully gang are sometimes amplified thanks to the diffusion of responsibility. Each individual in the group does not feel personally accountable for the bullying actions since the blame is shared among all members. Consequently, this can result in escalating levels of bullying, as each group member is encouraged to outshine the others as they compete for dominance.

The hidden impact of bullying

When we think about the negative repercussions of bullying, we tend to focus on the immediate effects on the victim in the incident. We might assume that, as soon as the bullying stops, then so do the effects. However, bullying usually has a far wider and longer-lasting impact, one that stays with the victim for years following the event.

The effect that my own little schoolhouse bully had on me became evident one day when I was a freshman in high school. I had a crush on a boy in my class. I used to spend the entire day dreaming about his eyes and staring at his perfect curls. He sat in front of me, so it was hard to stare at anything other than his head. One day, as I came back from the bathroom, I saw my crush bent over my backpack. In one second, all the memories of Freddy putting bugs and stolen lunch boxes in my bag came rushing back. I walked up to him with my fists clenched, ready to punch him right where it mattered! Luckily, as I was about to sucker-punch him, I noticed a red envelope in his hand. I looked at him with confusion in my eyes. "I'm sorry," he said with blushed cheeks. "I wanted to keep it as a surprise, but you caught me. Will you be my Valentine?"

Although it was quite harmless in this case, the impact of being bullied by Freddy was still with me. It can take years to heal from a bullying incident. The effects can last a lot longer than we might expect. And our mental health—always teetering on a delicate balance—is susceptible to the psychological perturbations incited by such trauma. Bullying can cause feelings of loneliness, depression, and anxiety. It can lead to violent outbursts of aggression, inciting us to transfer our pain onto the next poor soul. Bullying can lead to low self-esteem, which might cause the victim to question her strengths and focus on her weaknesses, prompting her to wonder if the bully might actually have a point when exclaiming her supposed incompetencies.

Additionally, bullying doesn't just affect the intended victim. It hurts those around her too. When I told my mom what was happening with Freddy, it had a far more profound effect on her than I realized at the time. I knew she was upset, but it wasn't until I had children that I discovered how deeply my mom had been hurt.

One morning, while chatting over coffee, she told me how it had taken her years to overcome the feeling that she had not been a better mother. She felt she had let me down on several occasions and that she often pondered the ways that she could have been more proactive when handling the many little quagmires of my childhood. She thought she was a failure, while I thought she was my hero. She had saved me from many awful situations, yet she felt she should have done more. My mom had been the collateral damage of bullying—unintended but just as real.

The point of this story is to convey that there is usually more than one victim of bullying. Often, someone we care about (like a parent or a sibling) may be experiencing the pain along with us—which is all the more reason to develop the skills needed to put a stop to the problem as soon as possible.

Ch. 2: Are you (or someone you love) in a toxic relationship?

Dealing with bullies is hard. But dealing with toxic people can be an even more difficult and nuanced challenge.

There's a difference between "being a bully" and "being toxic." Bullies necessarily have malicious intent. Their aim is to cause harm, gain power, or achieve some form of dominance over their victims. Bullying is an overt form of aggression and abuse, characterized by the bully's attempt to capitalize upon an imbalance of power.

Some toxic people are also *bullies*; they seek to manipulate the world around them via their malevolent machinations. However, not all toxic people intend to cause you harm any more than a puddle intends to get your socks wet. The puddle was just lying there. You're the one that stepped in it. A *passive* toxic person may act in ways that are damaging to you without even realizing it. The impetus of their behavior is not derived from a need for dominance or power but rather from their own insecurities, fears, or unresolved emotional issues.

Despite the question of whether you're dealing with an *aggressive* toxic person or a *passive* one, the results of their toxicity are the same. Interacting with them often leaves you feeling drained, anxious, or demoralized. They may even foster a dynamic of dependency, in which your self-esteem, emotional well-being, and perhaps even your bank account is tied to their whims. Whether they are cognizant of their toxicity or just plain blind to its effects, their actions have the same pernicious effects. Toxic people can erode your inner peace, your confidence, and your ability to thrive.

In this chapter, we will delve deeper into the various forms of toxicity and describe some ways that you might go about recognizing it in your relationships. We'll start by listing nine of such toxic personalities. Of course, these descriptions are based on common patterns of behavior and may not comprise the subject's entire mode of living nor define his or her complete character. These are mere tendencies. But by understanding such patterns, we can better position ourselves to mitigate any potential harm that might arise from such encounters.

9 Types of Toxic People

Type 1. The Controller

The controller does exactly what the name suggests: they try to *control* you. But, if you're over eighteen years of age, then only *you* are in control of your life. If someone tries to take away your autonomy and make all your life decisions for you, then this person may be a control freak. Such behaviors are commonly seen in overbearing mothers, domineering fathers, or overprotective husbands.

A controller may try to dictate everything from the clothes you wear, to the food you eat, to the friends you keep, to the career path you follow. In severe cases, they might even try to control your thoughts and feelings, invalidating your emotions and imposing their own viewpoint as the "correct" one. This intense need for control often stems from their own insecurities, fears, or a desire for power, and it can create a suffocating environment that stifles personal growth.

Type 2. The Debbie Downer

A 1968 Hanna-Barbera cartoon entitled "The Adventures of Gulliver" featured a very glum character who was appropriately named "Glum." In the show, Glum would humorously pronounce doom and gloom at every turn, no matter how trivial his current predicament was.

- "We're doomed."
- "It'll never work."
- "We're done for."
- "It's hopeless."

Such were the many mantras of Glum. This cartoon aired before my time. But fans of the show have put together some hilarious Glum montages on YouTube, which are worth checking out.

It's likely that you have a *Glum* in your life too. We've all come across a similarly pessimistic person, one who sees the negative side of every situation (even a fortuitous one). This type of person is more colloquially called a "Debbie Downer." While it's perfectly natural to feel down sometimes, it's quite another thing to perpetually pronounce your dissatisfaction to the world and dwell on the negative aspects of life while discarding all the positives. The *Debbie Downer* can drain your energy and lower your spirits with her incessant pessimism, thus making the maintenance of healthy relationships difficult.

Type 3. The Liar

Honesty, *trust*, and *respect* are three of the most basic and essential aspects of any relationship. Unfortunately, the lies people tell can break all three of these virtues in an instant, and often, the liar himself doesn't care. The problem with having a liar in your life is that you're never sure if he or she is telling the truth. This can make us paranoid. And can prompt us to second-guess every interaction we have—even with the non-liars in our life.

Type 4. The Perfectionist

The problem with the perfectionist is that even *they* aren't even good enough for themselves. So how can you ever hope to be good enough for them? The perfectionist believes that the only way to be "good" is to be "perfect." And they're inclined to demand the same level of performance from every person in their vicinity. Of course, the perfectionist fails to understand that *perfection is subjective*. They're convinced that they have stumbled upon the one true and proper way to live. And any questioning of their dogma will not be permitted.

Type 5. The Manipulator

The *manipulator* is similar to the *liar* archetype, except that they are often intrinsically endowed with a great deal of *emotional intelligence*, which they use to their advantage in deceptive and often injurious ways. Manipulators are experts at twisting situations, words, and actions to serve their own needs. They're skilled at bolstering their own narrative about how they are actually the hero of whatever quagmire they find themselves in. They have a unique ability to make someone else feel responsible for the outcome of their foibles, even if the accused party has nothing to do with it.

Type 6. The Cheater

Have you ever been the victim of cheating in a romantic relationship? A cheater is someone who betrays the trust of their significant other, typically via infidelity—violating the agreed-upon sexual boundaries of the relationship. While it's not uncommon for people to make mistakes in the game of love, chronic cheaters often exhibit patterns of deceit, a lack of accountability, and a blatant disregard for the feelings of their partner. This breach of trust can lead to severe emotional distress for the offended party.

Type 7. The Drunk

Alcohol has been a part of the human experience for a long time. Mankind has probably been distilling spirits since the advent of agriculture, perhaps dating as far back as 7,000 BC. This practice spread across cultures and continents, becoming ingrained in most aspects of society, from graduation ceremonies to religious rituals. Alcohol has surely played an important role in our cultural and even in our evolutionary history. However, with its widespread use came the potential for *misuse*. When consumption becomes excessive, it can transform an otherwise rational person into a fount of toxicity. The "mean drunk" archetype is a common trope, both in literature as well as in the lived experience of each of us. We all have a drunk uncle, friend, or cousin who has spent some time in rehab.

Dealing with the capricious emotions of an alcoholic can be taxing for everyone involved. It's a rollercoaster of unpredictability, often involving mood swings, aggressive behavior, or depressive episodes. A person who excessively drinks not only does irreparable physical harm to themselves but also to their strained relationships. Additionally, since alcohol is highly addictive, it can be extremely difficult for an alcoholic to halt his abusive behaviors, especially if he has a genetic predisposition that is forever calling upon him to take another drink.

Type 8. The Competitor

The competitor has to win. It doesn't matter what the nature of the contest is, nor is the value of the prize particularly important. Instead, the competitor just needs to know that he is the "winner" — that he stands victorious while everyone else is second best. Competitors like to enter competitions. But even if something isn't a competition, they'll turn it into one.

Now, there's nothing wrong with adopting a spirited persona and engaging in healthy competition among friends or family. But, when every single interaction becomes a test of "who is better," then such an aggressive approach to life can put a strain on relationships.

Type 9. The Insecure One

Some people are crippled by insecurity. They must continually seek out validation and reassurance from those around them, all because their self-esteem is so fragile. They constantly compare themselves to others. And they can never manage to feel comfortable enough to believe that they are deserving of the people in their lives. In romantic relationships, such insecurities often manifest in the form of jealousy, neediness, and a constant desire for their partner's approval. When they don't get immediate feedback in this domain, they might become manic with fear. And may elect to take out their emotions on the very person whom they crave affirmation from. Given that nobody can provide a stream of constant validation forever, a psychological outburst is all but inevitable. This degree of emotional dependency can be highly toxic to both parties.

Does any of the above sound familiar?

Have you ever encountered or witnessed any behaviors that are similar to the many types of toxic encounters that we have outlined in this chapter?

It's likely that you have.

We all have.

It's likely that this chapter reminds you of someone you know. Or brings back memories of a painful time in your life that you perhaps would rather forget...

We all know what it's like to lie in bed feeling wronged by someone whose toxicity has managed to permeate our mind. We've all dealt with the grief, frustration, and doubt that such interactions have caused. The scars left by such bouts of emotional turmoil cover sensitive wounds. If this section has been difficult to read, I do apologize. But it is only by familiarizing ourselves with the many forms of toxicity that we can begin to recognize the signs of a bad romance before it's allowed to evolved into an even worse relationship.

Seven signs that you're in a toxic relationship

Struggling with the affairs of the heart is never easy. When it comes to relationships, we all want to believe that our path in life will lead to a storybook ending. We want to believe that our chosen partner wants what's right for us. We want to believe in the power of love. This belief can sometimes blind us from the reality of our situation. We'll dismiss red flags, disregard sound advice, and rationalize away any suspect behavior that our partner engages in.

But living in denial can lead to more harm than good, perpetuating a cycle of pain, resentment, and disappointment.

To help you avoid this strife, we'll consider some of the tell-tale signs of a toxic relationship, discussing everything from the subtle hints to the more overt indicators of toxicity. By recognizing these signs early, you can take a step towards asserting your boundaries, breaking away from destructive patterns, and cultivating healthier (more loving) relationships.

Below, I've listed some signposts that might indicate if your relationship is toxic.

Sign 1: Hostile communication

This occurs when words, body language, or other nonverbal forms of communication are used to aggressively convey a threat to a partner. If there is regular hostile communication in a relationship then it's probably a toxic coupling. Watch out for the following behaviors:

- Yelling
- Name-calling or exchanging hurtful phrases
- Throwing objects and breaking things
- Physical intimidation or force
- Constant interrupting
- Frequent bouts of the "silent treatment"

Hostile communication can also occur in the form of passive-aggressive behavior. If your significant other only listens to you so that they can craft a witty retort, then they may not be truly listening to you at all (though they might insist that they are). In such a relationship, heated confrontations may result in you being *heard* but not *understood*. Such veiled hostilities might leave you feeling alone and hurt without truly understanding why.

Sign 2: Controlling behavior

Our *personal agency* is one of the few things in life that nobody can take from us. The ability to decide for ourselves is a precious gift and something we should never give up. When our partner tries to exercise dictatorial control over our lives, it is a sure sign of toxicity. There are many ways that the offending party might attempt such a ploy. Commonly, a carrot-and-stick methodology is used wherein rewards are dangled in front of the victim to incentivize compliance, and punishment is doled out for non-compliance. This tactic undermines the individual's autonomy and personal growth, creating a destructive cycle of dependence and fear. Other controlling behaviors a toxic person might engage in include:

- Dictating what the morally correct course of action is.
- Threatening to reveal your secrets.
- Keeping a log of everything you do or say.
- Managing all financial matters.
- Managing every interaction you have with other people.
- Insisting on being present when any other interaction with a third party is occurring.
- Pretending that you don't know what you're talking about and are unskilled in handling day-to-day matters.
- Requiring passwords to all personal devices and email accounts.

It's essential to recognize such tactics for what they are— manipulative tools in the hands of a controlling individual, designed to suppress your own desires for the sake of maintaining their power over you.

Sign 3: Feeling drained all the time

When was the last time you did something because *you* wanted to? Perhaps for no other reason than you "just felt like it?"

If the answer was, "Not in ages!" then there might be a problem. If you feel like the stress caused by a relationship is causing you to feel like you don't have the energy or willpower to focus on your usual activities, then your relationship might be toxic. Here are a few ways that such a bout of listlessness might manifest in your life:

- Not sleeping well.
- Not eating well.
- No longer participating in activities that once brought you joy.
- Experiencing feelings of isolation or withdrawal.
- Feeling a constant state of worry or anxiety.
- Struggling with feelings of worthlessness or self-doubt.
- Not connecting with your loved ones.
- Failing to attend to your personal hygiene.

Stress can make even simple tasks like grooming seem like too much effort. Toxic relationships can drain us to the point where we don't even want to see the people closest to us, sometimes for fear of their reprisal.

Sign 4: An inability to trust

The uneasiness caused by a persistent lack of trust can be shrouded and difficult to pinpoint. Sometimes, you might not know exactly why you can't trust someone. But the feeling persists. The quiet unease hangs in the ether, and it causes you to second-guess every action.

The problem is, without this crucial sense of trust, relationships don't work. If we can't trust those closest to us, then we'll never be able to rely on them when the slings and arrows of life are inevitably cast in our direction. Nor can we ever fully embrace the vulnerability of intimacy and surrender our love to them.

A *lack of trust* usually starts small. You might not want to reveal a deep insecurity or a personal secret. Later, you may stop sharing your opinion about anything at all, choosing to only convey how you truly feel during a heated argument. Whatever form your *lack of trust* takes, healthy relationships hinge upon a foundation of security. Without trust, this foundation cannot be properly constructed.

Sign 5: Frequent lying

We all tell little white lies sometimes. But when lying becomes habitual, it's a glaring red flag that you might be in a toxic relationship. Frequent lying erodes trust and creates an environment of doubt and uncertainty. A habitual liar might:

- Makeup stories to avoid taking responsibility for their actions.
- Break promises or fail to fulfill commitments.
- Deny the reality of the situation or insist that something didn't happen when you know it did.
- Make excuses for their behavior rather than owning up to their mistakes.

The liar aims to deceive by manipulating the truth to suit his own needs. Habitual lying often comes paired with other ailments like alcoholism or infidelity. A relationship plagued with lies is a breeding ground for toxicity, as it fosters a home life laden with mistrust and betrayal.

Sign 6: "All take and no give"

It is common for one member of a relationship to feel like they're doing all the work. In a well-balanced relationship, both partners must adopt a give-and-take dynamic—always pursuing reciprocity and compromise in an effort to nurture the bond between them. However, in a toxic relationship, one partner may be constantly drawing from the well of the other's emotional, physical, or financial resources, all without ever returning the favor. This can quickly lead to exhaustion and resentment for the benevolent member. Indicators that you might be in an "all take and no give" relationship include:

- An unwillingness in your partner to compromise about any decision.
- A strangling reliance on you for emotional support.
- Constantly borrowing money or demanding that you volunteer some other resource.
- Being quick to anger when they don't get their way.
- Failing to acknowledge or appreciate your efforts.

Such one-sided relationships can be draining and frequently result in one party feeling unappreciated and exploited. Mutual respect and reciprocity are key pillars in the formation of a healthy relationship. If these elements are missing, it might be time to reassess your situation.

Sign 7: A bevy of excuses

Are excuses the coin of the realm in your home?

- Do you feel as if you're always cleaning up after your partner's mistakes?
- Does he seem to be forever in a jam and completely reliant upon your charity to save him?
- Do you feel the need to always make excuses for him?
- Alternatively, does your significant other have a repertoire of excuses at the ready? And is he apt to select and use one of his excuses as effortlessly as a magician selects a card from a hat?

If your partner's tongue is a hotbed of excuses, then you might be in a toxic relationship. Often, the offending party doesn't recognize that their behavior is inappropriate, rude, or harmful. When confronted about their actions, they might be inclined to dismiss their behavior as being "just a joke." Or they might blame it all on stress, fatigue, or (quite commonly) alcohol. Other retorts might include:

- "You're the one who made me do it."
- "I wouldn't have reacted this way if you hadn't..."
- "You know I didn't mean it."
- "Can't you take a little criticism?"
- "You should know how I get when I'm like this."
- "You knew what I was like when you married me."

By rationalizing or downplaying their bad behaviors, *excuse makers* avoid taking responsibility for their actions. And when both parties in the relationship continue to make excuses for each other, then the cycle of toxicity continues indefinitely.

Rest assured that no excuse justifies emotional or physical harm. Everyone is responsible for their actions and the consequences that follow. No one has the right to treat you poorly, regardless of their justifications.

What to do when someone you love is in a toxic relationship

It is possible that you recognized some aspects of your own relationship (or that of a loved one) in our preceding list of red flags. Gauging the toxicity of a relationship can be worrying, particularly if you suspect that such toxic behaviors are currently affecting someone near and dear to your heart. Few things are more painful and frustrating than watching the slow deterioration of someone you love. We might feel the need to kick in their front door and release them from the prison of their own making. But we must remember that *they don't see what we see.*

- We see a toxic relationship that is sucking all the joy from their life. But they see the father of their children.
- We see a jerk who everyone dislikes. But they see the friend they've had since kindergarten.
- We see an emotionally abusive partner who constantly puts them down. But they see a person who is sometimes capable of great love.

The many heroes and villains that comprise the story of our lives are complicated characters. Often, discerning which party has the moral high ground is a challenging task. As a friend and a confidant, the scope of our job may be difficult to quantify. Our ability to provide aid may be limited. Sometimes all we can do is provide our loved ones with a safe space to express their thoughts and feelings. We must tread lightly, respecting their autonomy and personal boundaries while standing ready to aid them in their journey toward realizing the true nature of their relationship. Our role is not to force change or pass judgment but to be a beacon of understanding and empathy in what can be a very tumultuous and confusing time in their lives. Below, I've listed some tips that should help you navigate such interactions.

Tip 1: Keep making plans to see them

If you're dealing with someone in the grips of a harmful relationship, estranging them will probably only cause them to feel even *more* isolated and *more* dependent upon the toxic individual in their life. Regular contact allows you to maintain a relationship with them and keep an eye on their situation. Such encounters can provide an essential lifeline, reminding them of the love and respect they deserve and perhaps encouraging them to reconsider their current circumstances.

We often underestimate how restorative a little normalcy can be for someone who is in a dark place. Having a weekend of laughs and good memories might be just what the person needs to realize how much the bad relationship has affected her.

Remember, the purpose of instigating such a rendezvous is not to fix or break up the bad relationship. Instead, our initial goal is just to offer love and companionship to our friend. And attempt to indicate to them that we are willing to support them if, at some point, they make a decision to seek change.

Tip 2: Don't ask too many questions

When you sit down to talk with a close friend, it is common to inquire about her life. But if this friend is entangled in a toxic relationship, you may have to tread carefully around sensitive topics. You might be dying to know every detail about what's going on with their significant other. But inundating them with probing questions about an unhealthy relationship may come across as intrusive and cause them to push away. Instead, allow them to control the conversation and reveal information at their own pace. Make it clear that you're there to listen and support, not to interrogate. Express your concern but remember that they need to feel safe and understood, not judged or pressured. If they choose to open up about their relationship, listen attentively and respond empathetically. Validate their feelings and reassure them that they are not alone in their struggle. Be patient and be there for them when they decide it's time to talk. This will show them that you love and support them, making it far easier for them to reveal more to you in the future.

Tip 3: Don't badmouth the person they care about

When someone is harming a person you love, it can be difficult to bite your tongue and refrain from levying criticism toward the offending party. But such displays of patience may be essential. Here's why: There's a reason why they haven't left yet. They probably still love the person we hate. And badmouthing this person will likely just prompt them to get defensive and revert to attempting to explain away the malicious behavior. Instead, focus your energy on highlighting the positive aspects of your friend or family member rather than on disparaging the person who is causing them harm. Compliment them on their strength and resilience. Doing so can help them see their own worth, and they may eventually achieve a new perspective from which to objectively evaluate their present condition.

Tip 4: Express your opinion with empathy and compassion

When we find ourselves in a dark place—whether because of a toxic relationship, a bad habit, or poor life choices—then receiving a list of all the things that *other people* think we should do can seem aggressive and judgmental. A treatise about how poorly we've handled things will not always be received with grace. This might not be what the offended party needs right now.

So, when someone you love is suffering in a toxic relationship, be cautious with your willingness to dole out personal opinions and sage bits of advice. Take a breath before you share your feelings, and always do so with empathy. That means taking strides to second guess your emotions and mentally putting yourself in the shoes of someone who is currently suffering.

Remember, the word "compassionate" comes from the Latin term "*compati*," which means "to suffer with," not "to advise." Your righteous fury can wait until after the problem has been adequately resolved.

Tip 5: Help them see their worth

When helping someone navigate through a difficult situation, it can sometimes be useful to envision the hurt individual as they *were*, and not as they are now—in a betrodden and forlorn state. When out with your friend, you might try pretending that the toxic element of her relationship doesn't exist (at least not for the evening). Try to focus on your friend's gifts and talents. Recall all the things that attracted you to her when you first met. Try to bring up positive aspects of her life:

- Mention her passions or her career.

- Ask her about her past achievements and any new projects she might have on the horizon.
- Compliment her on her strengths and remind her of the times when she displayed courage and resilience.
- Reminisce over happy memories; laughter can be a powerful antidote to despair.

Such musings can serve as a reminder of what a healthy and supportive relationship looks like. Hopefully, by engaging in such exchanges, your friend might be in a better position to recognize the contrast between a positive interaction and the toxic encounter in which she is currently embroiled.

Tip 6: Be the rock in the relationship

In consideration of the proceeding items, you might notice that they all require a great deal of restraint and patience. You might also be thinking, "These tips don't actually solve the problems caused by my friend's toxic relationship…"

You're right about that.

Unless you're a clinical psychologist (with a license to lock someone up in a padded room), you cannot physically extract your friend from a toxic relationship. She has to make that decision all on her own. At the end of the day, it is up to *her* to decide who she will (and will not) allow into her life. All we can do is offer love, support, and advice when it is requested. Beyond that, our job primarily consists of being a "rock"—an immovable foothold that she can rely on whenever she loses her balance and starts to fall.

This road to recovery might be long and filled with numerous stumbles. But having a trusted friend by her side will undoubtedly make the journey more bearable. Have faith in your friend's capacity to overcome the obstacles she faces. Each small step towards self-realization may be hard won. But each step is a victory in itself. With the bond of friendship as her anchor, she will be in a better position to muster the courage needed to make the climb up the mountain of personal growth and freedom.

Ch. 3: How to spot and deal with a narcissist

With the advent of social media (particularly via "selfie culture" as presented on apps like TikTok, YouTube, and Facebook), it sometimes seems as though *everyone* is a narcissist these days. But the reality of the illness is far more complex than mere displays of vanity. In this chapter, we'll discuss the origins of the condition and talk about how you can identify and understand narcissistic behaviors among those you love. We'll also discuss the adverse effects that narcissism has on families and romantic relationships. Our objective is to enumerate some of the more curious facets of the condition, and also to provide some practical tools for managing narcissism in various contexts.

What is narcissism?

The term "narcissism" was derived from the Greek myth of *Narcissus*, the young hunter from Thespiae who fell in love with his own reflection. Narcissism is one of the most familiar psychological disorders, often discussed in popular magazines and media websites. The classic symptoms of narcissism are frequently depicted in movie characters, typically with a comical twist. Think of:

- Miranda Priestly in *The Devil Wears Prada,*
- Scar in *The Lion King,*

- Gordon Gekko in *Wall Street,*
- or, Regina George in *Mean Girls.*

Yet, despite its prevalence in popular culture, there is still a huge lack of understanding about the symptoms and causes of narcissism, as well as an inability for normal people to comprehend the amount of damage that a single narcissist can do. It's been estimated that as many as 1 out of every 200 people in the United States are narcissists, and the overwhelming majority of them are male. So, if you had the opportunity to interact with at least 200 people last year, then, chances are, you have already exchanged some words with a narcissist.

Defining Narcissism

Narcissism can be broadly defined as excessive self-love, admiration, or self-centeredness. It is important to distinguish between *self-esteem* and *pathological narcissism*. High self-esteem is crucial for maintaining a healthy and positive persona, while pathological narcissism is characterized by an inflated sense of self and an inability to empathize with others. For the narcissist, the planets revolved around him. The objects of the cosmos are there to be manipulated or exploited for his own desires. And when the planets do not align to the narcissist's liking, the perceived slight to his grandiose designs can lead to bouts of intense anger and rage, all directed at those he perceives as being the cause of the disorder. This underscores the inherent volatility and destructiveness of pathological narcissism, making it a complex and challenging issue to treat and manage.

What Causes Narcissism?

It is impossible to pinpoint any specific causes that lead to the development of any given personality disorder, as they are formed by many factors that are difficult to account for. That said, genetics, environment, and neurobiology surely play a role in the development of the condition. We'll discuss each factor briefly now.

1. Genetics

Your DNA affects more than just your hair color. Genetics seems to influence the development of narcissistic personality disorder. Some of the traits passed on from parent to child are the sense of grandiosity and entitlement, both of which are prevalent in narcissistic behavior. Indeed, some studies have evidenced a high heritability rating for narcissistic traits, suggesting that genetics could account for up to 50% of the variance. It's important to note, however, that if you manage to discover a narcissist in your family tree, this does not necessarily mean you will inevitably develop the disorder.

2. Environment

When it comes to narcissism, *nurture* may be as important as nature. In this case, "nurture" refers to early childhood experiences, the dynamics of the parent-child relationship, and any possible traumatic events experienced during the younger years. Furthermore, it seems that narcissism can develop in some people who have received high levels of unjustified parental adoration or harsh criticism.

3. Neurophysiology

Researchers have also discovered a connection between narcissism and certain types of brain activity. Patients with narcissism have an underdeveloped *anterior insula*—the part of the brain linked to emotions such as compassion and empathy. This abnormal activity perhaps amplifies their narcissistic behaviors, such as acting without taking into consideration the feelings of others and discarding the protests of those who are the victims of their actions.

The Symptoms of Narcissism

Only a qualified health professional can confirm a positive diagnosis of *narcissistic personality disorder (NPD)*. Yet, it is possible to identify a candidate for the condition by observing their behavior. If you recognize one or more of the following traits, then you might want to pursue professional help to determine if your partner or family member has NPD.

Trait #1: A distorted perception of self-importance

Narcissists have a warped view of their importance or authority, often viewing themselves as superior to those around them. Although they do not necessarily feel universally superior in every aspect of their lives, they may maintain a default sense of superiority and importance in whatever interaction they stumble into.

Trait #2: Expecting special treatment

Due to their distorted perception of themselves, a narcissist expects special treatment from everyone wherever they go. They demand favor, rarely apologize, and believe everyone should comply with their wishes. This is the cause of much friction in the lives of those who are unfortunate enough to be in the narcissist's orbit. Family members are often expected to cater to the narcissist's needs, despite how haughty his requests might be.

Trait #3: Demanding attention

Narcissists thrive in the spotlight of social attention, and they might insist on being the topic of conversation. They will sometimes interject their opinions into a discourse, even if their opinion is unwarranted, just to ensure that all eyes are on them, and that their presence in the room is known.

Trait #4: Living in a fantasy world of success and power

The narcissistic mind is often consumed by exaggerated images and visualizations portraying their immense power and beauty. They like the feeling of being in control, not only of their own lives but also of the lives of others. If reality is perceived as a threat to their elevated worldview, then reality can be swiftly ignored.

Trait #5: An inability to take criticism

Narcissists don't like criticism. When receiving any form of critique, they might react defensively (even aggressively), perceiving the retort as a personal attack against their wellbeing. This is due to their inflated self-perception and their need to maintain an idealized vision of themselves. Since they often don't perceive anything to be their fault, they may genuinely not believe that they are ever deserving of censure.

Trait #6: A willingness to take advantage of others

To a narcissist, every person in their life simply exists as a steppingstone that paves the route to achieving their own desires. Hence, they have little hesitation in abusing or manipulating others for personal gain. The narcissist might use tactics such as emotional manipulation or exploitation to bolster their own self-importance or pursue their own self-interests.

Trait #7: Extreme arrogance

Considering all the symptoms we've discussed thus far, it shouldn't be surprising that narcissists can be quite arrogant. Their inflated ego prompts them to act superior and look down upon their friends, family members, or coworkers. This arrogance can manifest in many ways, including a patronizing attitude, dismissive behavior towards ancillary opinions, or an inability to accept critique or correction. Sometimes, vanity takes hold; narcissists might insist on dressing in designer brands and driving luxury cars to flaunt their status. Such props are useful in their never-ending quest to appear superior to everyone else.

The 6 Different Types of Narcissists

Not all narcissists behave in the same way. Nor do they have precisely the same indicators of their condition. In the broader umbrella of narcissism, researchers have noted six distinct subtypes. Each subtype is characterized by unique traits that will help you to distinguish what sort of narcissist you might be dealing with. Below, I've listed a description of each type. By reviewing this taxonomy, we hope to add some context to the complexity and nuance involved with identifying the particulars of the disorder.

Type 1: Malignant Narcissism

The *malignant narcissist* exhibits the most severe symptoms of the disorder. Their displays of narcissism are obvious and extreme, typically paired with antisocial behavior, vindictiveness, paranoia, aggression, and even sadism. Additionally, the ailment commonly causes them to portray symptoms of other mental health disorders, such as antisocial personality disorder and borderline personality disorder, making them somewhat dangerous to have in your life.

Type 2: Antagonistic Narcissism

Does the narcissist in your life thrive on competition and rivalry? If so, then it is likely that they fall into this subtype. The antagonistic narcissist is highly competitive, easily stirred to anger, and willing to engage in confrontation to achieve a victory, no matter how inconsequential the contest is. Winning is very important to them. And they'll take advantage of others to get to the top.

Type 3: Covert Narcissism

While narcissism is linked with a high sense of superiority, the covert narcissist shows excessive behavior in an entirely different direction. Narcissists who fall into this category can be difficult to identify. They seemingly have low self-esteem and can be very introverted, which is in stark contrast to the charismatic narcissist trope that is so common in popular portrayals of the disorder. The covert narcissist is insecure and defensive. He might struggle with anxiety and depression, and may avoid any interaction with the potential to trigger these symptoms. Such narcissists still primarily concentrate on themselves and fail to value the feelings of others, but their focus might be only on their own inefficiencies.

Type 4: Overt Narcissism

This is the subtype most commonly linked to narcissism in the public eye. They live a life of grandiosity and portray behavior classified as overbearing, arrogant, competitive, entitled, and outgoing. They are the ones who display every classic symptom of narcissism, and they love feeling good about themselves so much that they are willing to manipulate and take advantage of others to enjoy this satisfaction. Overt narcissists constantly overestimate their own popularity, intelligence, attractiveness, and abilities.

Type 5: Somatic Narcissism

While all narcissists lack depth, the *somatic narcissist* is probably the shallowest of them all. Their entire sense of grandiosity is based on the appeal of their outer appearance. They link their sense of superiority solely to their looks, weight, muscle mass, and sex appeal. They consider themselves above all others in this regard and won't hesitate to harshly criticize people based on physical features that the narcissist considers important.

Type 6: Communal Narcissism

This type is the opposite of the antagonistic narcissist since they attach a high value to fairness. They are the ones who are altruistic heroes in their own eyes and would blow their tops when they witness what they perceive as moral inequities. Given such behaviors, it's easy to assume that their intensions are good and that they genuinely care for people. However, their interest in preserving rights and values is not guided by their moral compass but is instead intended to increase their sense of importance and to gain the admiration of others.

Exploring the Dark Triad

The *dark triad* is a term coined by psychologists Delroy L. Paulhus and Kevin M. Williams in 2002. It refers to a sinister trifecta of personality traits, namely:

- Narcissism,
- Psychopathy,
- and Machiavellianism.

Each disorder is referred to as being "dark" because the afflicted subject is prone to engage in wicked and malevolent behaviors. It's useful to consider each facet of the triad since there is so much overlap between the three. In this chapter, we have already discussed the first item on the list (narcissism). Now, let's sketch out the other two (psychopathy and Machiavellianism).

Dark Triad Component 1: Psychopathy

Of the three disorders linked to the Dark Triad, those who are psychopathic are the most malevolent. Psychopathy has similar roots to sociopathy. But psychopaths may be less reckless and impulsive. They're willing to be patient and "do the math." They're able to coldly calculate a plan of action for achieving their ruthless goals. The defining trait of a psychopath is a distinct lack of empathy. Indeed, they may not even be physically capable of empathizing, and they might be entirely devoid of a conscience. Psychopaths are not always violent, but they can be if violence is the key to achieving a particular goal.

Dark Triad Component 2: Machiavellianism

Niccolò di Bernardo dei Machiavelli (born 1469) was an Italian diplomat and philosopher from Florence, Italy. His political treatise, "The Prince," has been long regarded as a guidebook for power-hungry politicians. It prescribes the use of manipulation and deceit to seek out political influence. Thus, someone who is said to be engaging in *Machiavellian behavior* is utilizing subterfuge for personal gain, often with little regard for the ethical implications of their actions. Disciples of Machiavelli might be characterized by:

- A steadfast commitment to their own self-interests and personal goals.

- A tendency to invest in personal relationships via strategic calculation.
- A willingness to exploit others for personal gain.
- And an inflated sense of self-entitlement.

As you can see, Machiavellianism is closely related to Narcissism and Psychopathy. But it is distinct in its emphasis on calculated manipulation and strategic maneuvering to gain power.

Reviewing our Terms

In popular culture, psychology terminology is often thrown about haphazardly. And most people are not aware of the subtle differences between the varied facets of the dark triad. So let's take a moment to review a few psych terms. We'll start with three common conditions:

- A **"psychotic"** person is someone suffering from the symptoms of *psychosis*.
- A **"sociopath"** is someone who is suffering from the condition of *sociopathy*.
- A **"psychopath"** is someone suffering from the condition of *psychopathy*.

As with most mental conditions, the symptoms displayed by the subject can have a lot of overlap. We'll outline some of the more nuanced differences now:

- A **psychotic** person is not in touch with reality. The terms "psychotic" or "psychosis" sound similar to the term "psychopath," so people often get them confused. But psychosis is just one symptom of many mental health conditions, including schizophrenia, bipolar disorder, and depression. A person having a *psychotic episode* may be experiencing *hallucinations* or hold on to *delusional beliefs* about reality, insisting that their conception of the world is true despite any evidence to the contrary.

- A **sociopath** is a person who may be commonly diagnosed with *Antisocial Personality Disorder* (ASPD) — which means that they consistently display reckless behavior that does not conform to social norms or laws. They might be willing to engage in opportunistic criminal activity or even impulsive acts of physical assault for seemingly no reason at all. E.g., a sociopath might enjoy the thrill of pushing someone over just to watch them fall. Of course, this doesn't mean that they'll assault everyone in their proximity; they can sometimes empathize with close friends and family members. Sociopathy is not typically considered *innate* in the way psychopathy is. Instead, it is viewed as a result of the failure of society (or the family) to create a positive nurturing environment during early childhood development.

- A **psychopath** may also be diagnosed with *Antisocial Personality Disorder*. They are willing to break laws or engage in destructive behavior if doing so results in personal gain. What often distinguishes psychopaths from sociopaths is the origin of the illness. Psychopaths seem to be "born that way" (due to genetics) or perhaps "formed that way" (due to childhood trauma that occurs very early in life). Additionally, psychopaths may not always be mere opportunistic criminals—willing to hold up a liquor store or kidnap the woman they desire. Instead, many psychopaths are highly intelligent and calculating connivers, often willing to "play the long game" — crafting grand schemes to pursue their interests while treating everyone around them like pawns on a chessboard. The term **"psycho"** is just an abbreviated form of the word "psychopath." But it's often incorrectly used in popular culture to simply denote anyone who is acting crazy at the moment.

- A **narcissist** is a person diagnosed with *Narcissistic Personality Disorder* (NPD). This condition causes them to have an inflated sense of their own importance, an insufferable need for attention and admiration, and an inability to empathize with others. Unlike psychopaths (who may not feel anything when rejected), the self-esteem of a narcissist is fragile, and they may respond poorly to even the mildest bout of criticism. Their behavior focuses on maintaining an inflated image of themselves rather than on manipulating others for the mere thrill of asserting control.

Narcissists and Relationships

In glancing at our proceeding list of Dark Triad components, it is likely that many of the above-described traits remind you of someone you know. Remember, only a professional can diagnose someone with psychopathy, sociopathy, or narcissistic personality disorder. So don't be too quick to assign a label to each of your partner's inadequacies. Still, it is useful to familiarize yourself with the many ailments of the mind. People predisposed to Dark Triad traits are more likely to commit crimes, foster societal problems, and cause emotional harm to those around them. These traits can manifest in various forms of destructive behavior, from psychological manipulation to physical harm. Thus, if your partner does have one of these conditions, then your ability to recognize these traits might aid in nurturing an understanding of the impetus of their actions. Additionally, by developing the ability to notice these traits early, you'll be in a better position to erect relationship boundaries or seek out professional help if you suspect that someone you love might have one of these conditions.

Unfortunately, it is not uncommon for someone to be entangled in a relationship for several years before realizing that their partner is a narcissist. If you are currently in such a relationship, you may notice that your significant other often fails to take any sincere interest in the lives of anyone but themselves. And yet, your spouse may sometimes be capable of coming across as the most caring and giving partner in the world. He might even be inclined to shower you with gifts or words of adoration. Narcissists can be quite charming. However, due to his inability to experience genuine empathy, he will be unable to keep up this facade forever. The cracks in his faux finish will eventually appear, though perhaps not until significant emotional damage has been done.

Such scenarios often prompt one of the partners to wonder if a narcissist is capable of returning the love that they are so willing to share with them. Only a therapist could attempt to answer this question for your specific situation, and, even then, only after going to great lengths to analyze the degree of narcissism that your partner is inflicted with. If your partner truly has a neurological condition that prevents them from forming a genuine emotional connection, then conventional love may not be possible, though admiration, respect, and mutual understanding might still be cultivated over time. In any case, it is crucial to seek professional advice if you find yourself in a relationship with someone displaying narcissistic traits.

There is no cure for narcissism. But once the person has been diagnosed, they can get involved in one of several therapy programs that can help to mitigate the symptoms of the condition. Generally, the less *severe* their symptoms are, the more *positive* the results of the therapy will be. If you are currently in a relationship with a narcissist, then your best course of action is to learn all you can about the ailment and take the initiative in establishing the boundaries and norms by which your relationship can proceed. Though every life situation is unique, I've listed some general tips here that should aid in this process.

Boundary 1: Communication

Remember, since narcissists lack empathy, they often communicate with a blatant disregard for the feelings or perspectives of others. This can come in the form of belittlement, ignoring, or outright dismissing your presence in a conversation. In response to such behavior, make it clear to your significant other that such types of discourse are not acceptable. Be assertive but not confrontational. Clearly state your feelings and insist that you do not tolerate disrespectful or harmful language. An example of such a boundary might be to state:

I don't appreciate it when you talk to me so disrespectfully. If you do it again, I'll excuse myself from the conversation until you can speak to me with respect.

Often, narcissists will try to downplay their behavior or make it seem as though you're overreacting. Persistently outlining your boundaries—making known what is and isn't acceptable communication—will either force your partner to change his behavior or indicate to you that respectable communication with this person might not be feasible.

Boundary 2: Discretion

It is important to bear in mind that narcissists are not above using personal information to their advantage, perhaps for manipulation or even emotional abuse. Often, they will try to downplay their intrusion into your personal affairs. And, if they encounter any opposition to their queries, they might accuse *you* of being the secretive and untrustworthy one.

To establish rules for discretion, make it clear that your personal matters are just that—they are *personal*. It's fine to share experiences and thoughts with your partner, but you have the right to keep certain bits of information to yourself. Reinforce this boundary by politely declining to volunteer sensitive information that you'd rather keep private. And, when revealing intimate details, consider prefacing your remarks with a statement such as:

My feelings are private, and you can't share them with anyone else. I respect your privacy and consider our conversations confidential, and I expect you'll do the same.

Boundary 3: Financial independence

Since *financial control* is one of the common methods that narcissists use to control their partners, it may be crucial to maintain separate finances, accounts, and credit cards. This ensures that your own personal finances are not under the control of the narcissist in your life. Be prepared to state clearly,

I have a right to manage my own money, and I expect you to respect that.

If you must share resources or expenses with the narcissist, then make sure to have a written agreement (not just an oral one) about who is responsible for which assets. Establishing this boundary is not just about protecting your financial future, it's about preserving your personal autonomy and independence as well.

Boundary 4: Maintain your own personal space

At times, the presence of a narcissist in your life can become overwhelming, and you may need some *alone time* to emotionally recharge. Dealing with narcissists can be psychologically draining. Retreating to a personal space will allow you to rejuvenate and regain your peace of mind. Set up a space where you can isolate yourself from other negative influences on your state of mind, or where you can work on your own hobbies and interests without interruption. Assert your needs by clearly expressing yourself, saying:

I value my personal time and space for self-reflection. When I am in my personal space, I would appreciate it if you respect my privacy.

Boundary 5: Report sexual or physical abuse

Obviously, you can't tolerate physical or sexual abuse in your home. If this is occurring, then you must take the necessary measures to get yourself out of the situation as soon as possible. Any form of abuse is a serious topic. If your partner becomes abusive, it is crucial that you contact the proper authorities and take measures to protect yourself. Reporting these incidents not only helps preserves your safety but can also legally hold the abuser accountable for their actions.

How to avoid relationships with narcissists

Familial obligations sometimes call upon us to maintain a relationship with a narcissist or a psychopath, even if we don't want to. E.g., if your child has been diagnosed as such, then learning to cope with his proclivities may be a lifelong endeavor. However, when it comes to the *affairs of the heart*, interactions with narcissists might best be avoided. It is common for a woman to have a bad romantic experience with a narcissist, and then seek to avoid making the same mistake twice. If you think you might be courting a man with narcissistic tendencies, then here are a few red flags to look out for.

Tip 1: Go slow

Don't rush the courtship process. Gather as much information as you can about your dating partner. Ask them questions and listen attentively to their response. If you begin to notice any of the telltale signs of narcissism that we have discussed in this chapter (such as a constant need for admiration, a lack of empathy, or manipulative behavior), then it may be wise to reconsider the relationship.

Tip 2: Keep your friends close

Narcissists often try to discourage their romantic partners from having relationships that don't involve them. They might claim that your friends and family don't understand you the way they do. Or they might become jealous of the time you spend with them. Maintain your existing relationships and confide in your trusted friends about any concerns you may have about your new partner. Their outside perspective can aid in your efforts to spot the signs of narcissism.

Tip 3: Pay attention to the details during each conversation

Remember, narcissists are master manipulators. And their best weapon is their tongue. *Gaslighting* is a deception tactic wherein the conspirator makes their victim question their reality, memory, or perceptions. The term originates from the 1944 film "Gaslight," in which a husband attempts to trick his wife into believing that she's losing her mind. If your new romantic partner seems to contradict, deny, or dismiss your rendition of past experiences, then this may be a sign that they're trying to gaslight you. Narcissists employ this technique to cause their partner to doubt their faculties, thus making the victim more reliant upon the narcissist's curated version of reality. If you continually feel misunderstood or confused when discussing past events or disagreements with your partner, then such a red flag might indicate a tendency towards narcissistic behavior.

Tip 4: Trust your instincts

The human brain is a complex computer, tuned via millions of years of evolution. Your ancestors had to be good at spotting a bad thing when they saw one. If they weren't good at it, they wouldn't be around long to tell anyone about their mistake. What we colloquially call a "gut instinct" is actually your mind's way of processing subtle cues and excreting an emotional response based on its calculations of this data. Of course, this all happens at a subconscious level. Thus, if you consistently feel uneasy around your new partner, then consider heeding these perturbations of the mind. Such sensations might be your brain's way of warning you about the potential danger of continuing on your present course with this new love interest.

Get the Worksheet

If you haven't downloaded my free worksheet yet, browse over to get it now. Inside, you'll find a brief quiz which attempts to help you determine if your partner has narcissistic tendencies.

If you're reading this book on a Kindle or an iPad, you can click the link below. Or, paperback readers can type the link into your iPhone or PC.

www.tiny.cc/bullyguide

Ch. 4: How to spot and deal with a pathological liar

Some people we encounter in this world have a tendency to bend the facts, exaggerate stories, or fabricate their own version of past events. Or, to put it more bluntly, some people like to *lie*. Interacting with such individuals can be challenging, especially if we're forced to mingle in their proximity—i.e., if the person is a coworker, family member, or even a romantic partner. Compulsive liars cast us in a perpetual state of skepticism. Relationships are built on trust. But if you can't trust a word that comes out of your partner's mouth, then the relationship can never progress.

Pathological lying is a complex behavior often linked to various antisocial and borderline personality disorders. It's characterized by a compulsive urge to lie, often for personal gain but sometimes for no apparent reason whatsoever. Some people with this condition can weave intricate webs of deceit, creating a false reality that is difficult to untangle. When they're skilled at their craft, their lies can seem quite believable, further complicating the process of distinguishing truth from fiction. Unlike the occasional white lies that most of us let drop every now and then, pathological lying is a chronic habit of dishonesty that develops into a core aspect of the liar's psyche.

In this chapter, we'll delve into the intricacies of pathological lying and discuss the impact it has on our interpersonal relationships. We'll explore the psychological underpinnings of the condition and discuss the many challenges that can arise when dealing with a friend or family member who is prone to engage in bouts of serial lying. Coping with the condition requires empathy, patience, assertiveness, and possibly professional intervention. But by shedding some light on the disease, we hope to equip ourselves to recognize the signs of pathological lying and manage its effects.

The Signs of Pathological Lying

If you've ever had to reside with or work with a pathological liar, then the symptoms of the condition are likely already well-known to you. Pathological liars lie a lot. But, the more time we spend with them, the more skilled we become at deciphering their deceit. Even the craftiest liar usually can't keep a complex charade going for very long. With each turn of the clock, more facets of their fanciful stories are divulged, eventually revealing a complex mosaic of their distorted reality.

Let's list four symptoms of the condition now.

1. Consistent inconsistencies

Consistent contradictions are one of the most telling signs of a pathological liar. They alter their stories or give contradicting facts in a way that makes it challenging for the listener to construct a coherent narrative. This confabulation of past events may reoccur in multiple aspects of their life, including intimate relationships, everyday occurrences, and personal experiences. Discrepancies are most easily spotted when observing a pathological liar telling a story to two different people. In such circumstances, it's often quite easy to pick up on the inconsistencies between the actual events and the liar's retelling of the events, particularly if you were present to witness the story's origin.

2. Exaggeration and fabrication

Exaggeration and fabrication are common tactics used by pathological liars to improve upon or spice up their tales. To impress or win sympathy, they might embellish facts, emphasize their own role in the narrative, or invent totally fictitious incidents. Their stories can be so intricate and comprehensive that it can be difficult to tell what is real and what is fantasy. When monitoring a recounting by a pathological liar, keep an eye out for flamboyant exaggerations and examine their retelling carefully to look for attention-seeking behaviors or a need for social affirmation. Furthermore, it's a good idea to keep a "plausibility meter" running in the back of your mind. If there are too many grandiose elements in their story (i.e., if their story doesn't pass a "sanity check"), then such red flags may indicate the presence of a serial liar.

3. A Lack of remorse

When confronted about their lying, pathological liars frequently exhibit little remorse or guilt. When their deceptions are discovered, they might act casually or even deny any wrongdoing. Alternatively, they may not even react at all. If you bring up any evidence that reveals their inconsistencies, it might simply be ignored. No two people react the same way after being accused of a lie. Taking note of exactly how this reaction plays out, and comparing the reaction to other patterns of behavior is one way to tell if you're dealing with a pathological liar or not.

4. A tendency to change the subject quickly

Pathological liars are quite willing to drop a conversation thread when they see that it's no longer of benefit to them. If they receive too many questions about a particular event, they might attempt to switch topics or divert attention to something else. This is an evasion tactic used to avoid being caught in a lie or to escape from having to explain any inconsistencies in their tale. When backed into a corner, they might resort to noting distractions (like insisting that they have an incoming text on their cellphone) or they might attempt to steer the conversation into the uncharted waters of a completely new (and likely fabricated) topic. They do this with the hope that their little smokescreen will confuse their listener, at least enough to keep up the *"lie of the day"* for a little while longer.

5. Manipulative behavior

Some liars lie because it works for them. Pathological liars might engage in their deceitful behavior because they know that their tall tales sometimes result in a bountiful payoff. These individuals master the art of pulling on heartstrings, creating dramatic narratives, and presenting themselves as the hero (or the victim) in their narrative, all in an effort to garner favor from their mark. They might even resort to flattery, charm, or emotional manipulation to get what they want. So, when dealing with a liar, be on the lookout for any indication that they might be attempting to utilize deceit to manipulate the people in their orbit for personal gain.

The Causes of Pathological Lying

Now that we've talked about the symptoms of pathological lying, let's talk about the causes. While research is still underway, some elements that may have an impact on the emergence of this behavior have been identified. It's vital to remember that these elements are not always mutually exclusive and that a mixture of them may lead to pathological lying in certain people. We'll list five of the frequently acknowledged causes now.

Cause 1. Underlying psychological conditions
Some mental health problems, such as narcissistic personality disorder, borderline personality disorder, or antisocial personality disorder, have been linked to pathological lying. A warped sense of self, a need for attention or validation, and a lack of empathy may be characteristics of these illnesses, all of which can fuel the urge to lie.

Cause 2. Low self-esteem
People with low self-esteem may utilize lying tactics to construct an idealized self-image or to win the approval and respect of others. To make up for feelings of inadequacy or uncertainty, they fabricate stories about their accomplishments. And since the level of interest or admiration of their listener correlates with the grandeur of the tale, the compulsive liar is encouraged to compose ever more grandiose narratives, mostly as a way of soothing their low self-esteem or bolstering their ego.

Cause 3. Negative childhood experiences
Traumatic childhood experiences, such as abuse, neglect, or inconsistent parenting, can have a profound effect on a person's psychological growth. In response to these negative events, a person may develop a lying habit that enables them to escape from or alter reality. Their predilection for lying might develop in adolescence, used as a means of avoiding physical punishment or placating the abusive people in their lives.

Cause 4. Attention-seeking behavior

Some pathological liars use persistent dishonesty to get people's attention and provoke responses. Even if it involves lying to those around them, they might seek the approval, empathy, or adoration that they garner from their whimsical tales. For those individuals, who view any attention as a positive, lying becomes a crutch to obtain their proverbial fix. This thrill might be derived from self-aggrandizement or from painting someone else in a bad light. Such drama-seeking behavior might be summed up via the adage, "There is no such thing as bad publicity."

Cause 5. Habit

Pathological lying may develop from a learned behavior that is sustained and rewarded over time. A person may be more likely to lie if they repeatedly succeed in getting away with it or if they benefit from the deception in some way. This could stem from either lying to get out of some form of obligation, avoiding some form of punishment, or simply getting their way. The act of achieving positive outcomes to their lying behavior feeds the habit loop in their mind, thus further engraining the process of habitual lying.

Strategies for dealing with a pathological liar

Living with a pathological liar can be quite a challenge. The constant distortion of facts and bending of reality can leave one feeling disoriented, suspicious, and emotionally drained. If your current living situation demands that you share a floor with a pathological liar, then it may be in your interest to review some coping strategies that will help you to navigate through such a complex and emotionally taxing environment. I've listed several tips below.

Tip 1: Get used to asking for evidence

Pathological liars can't be trusted. So don't. Instead, get used to asking for proof of their activities whenever possible. For example, if you give the liar in your home some money to go out and pick up a pizza, then insist that he return with both the pizza as well as the receipt. If the receipt and half the money somehow miraculously disappear during the exchange, then inform the liar that he will not be allowed to eat any pizza. By putting the onus of proof on the pathological liar, you'll be creating a system of accountability, which should help to maintain transparency and aid in teaching the liar about the importance of truthfulness and the consequences that follow deceitful behavior.

Tip 2: Make sure that each lie is met with a penalty

Often, we can never know if the pathological liar in our life is telling the truth or not. But we can set up systems (such as the pizza receipt rule discussed above) that can aid in ensuring that certain procedures must be followed in order for us to believe the words coming from the liar's mouth. If you spot a discrepancy between the liar's words and the events that actually took place, then consequences must ensue. In our prior example, the consequence of lying was that the family member would not receive any pizza. Of course, the consequences that you employ will vary depending on the type of relationship you have with the liar in your life, as well as their age and the degree to which they are prone to engage in lying behavior.

Regardless of the type of consequences you employ, it's important to understand that *consistency* and *toughness* are essential in driving the message home and ensuring that a negative signal is associated with the act of lying. Over time, this can act as a deterrent, making the liar think twice before resorting to their habit of deceit.

Bear in mind, this is not about punishing the individual out of malice or anger, but about creating an environment where *honesty* is incentivized, and *deception* is discouraged. The ultimate goal is to help the pathological liar understand the negative implications of their actions, which will ideally foster a greater inclination towards truthfulness and personal integrity.

Tip 3: Avoiding engaging in shouting arguments or debates

When communicating with a pathological liar, breathe deeply, speak clearly, and react thoughtfully, always concentrating on the facts rather than on any emotions that might be bubbling up inside you. Getting into a heated argument about *the truth* with a pathological liar is not a fruitful discourse because they don't value the truth. Indeed, the very reason that they lied in the first place might be to merely bask in the thrill of watching you explode like a volcano. So don't partake in their games. Instead, maintain your composure, focusing on logic and reason. If you sense that the conversation is getting heated, then take a step back. It's okay to disengage and continue the conversation at a later date. This not only protects your own emotional well-being but also sends a strong message to the pathological liar that their attempts at manipulation and provocation have failed. When you do return to the conversation, focus on the need for evidence of the liar's truth claims, and penalties for lying, as discussed in the previous section. Clearly describe which set of behaviors are unacceptable and remind the liar of the consequences for breaking the rules.

Reinforcing boundaries helps build a sense of accountability and signals that dishonesty will not be accepted.

Tip 4: Cultivate compassion

While living with a compulsive liar might be distressing, try to remember that they're trapped in a pattern of pathological behavior that they may not be able to fully understand or control. Just as you would show empathy towards someone battling a physical illness, apply the same understanding to someone struggling with a mental one. This does not mean condoning or ignoring their harmful behavior, but rather, making an effort to empathize with their internal struggle, which can guide your responses and interactions with them in a healthier, more productive way. This level of compassion can also help safeguard your emotional well-being, as it reduces the likelihood that you might internalize their actions and feel personally attacked.

Tip 5: Seek out help and support

When dealing with pathological liars, it is crucial to get support from reliable friends and family, who are aware of your loved one's condition and who can, at the least, provide a sympathetic ear when times get tough. Merely talking about your feelings and experiences won't solve your problems. But it can lighten your emotional burden and provide some much-needed perspective to your woes. Moreover, having a strong support network can also help to reaffirm your understanding of the *actual reality*, not the one concocted by the pathological liar in your life.

As with every mental disorder, don't be afraid to seek out professional help when your loved one's condition becomes intolerable. Mental health professionals are trained to help you manage such conditions, and they understand the burden that family members must bear when coping with the disease. Psychological interventions such as Cognitive Behavioral Therapy (CBT) can be very helpful in changing the thought patterns that lead to pathological lying. Therapy is not a quick fix but a journey that requires patience, commitment, and consistent effort. But with time, it can provide the tools necessary to manage the condition and improve the quality of life for everyone involved.

Tip 6: Don't take their lying personally

In this chapter, we have discussed some of the root causes of pathological lying. For some who are inflicted with the condition, their tendency to fabricate or exaggerate reality might be innate. Their lies might be a manifestation of deeper psychological issues rather than a calculated intention to harm or mislead. This does not excuse their behavior, but it should help you to rationalize the disease.

It is natural to become offended when someone attempts to deceive you. However, if you're dealing with a compulsively lying family member whose condition stems from a deeply ingrained pathology, then it is crucial to keep reminding yourself that their dishonesty is probably not a reflection of your failure as a mother, partner, or friend. Instead, their incessant need to lie is the result of a complex psychological disorder that they're currently battling. While this realization may not always ease the hurt caused by their lies, it can aid in preventing you from taking it personally.

Living with a pathological liar can be exhausting. At times, some degree of *emotional detachment* may be necessary to get through the day. Developing stable boundaries to shield yourself from emotional manipulation is vital if you wish to maintain your mental health. Remember, emotional detachment in this context doesn't mean that you don't care. Instead, your willingness to tolerate your family member's deceit is a sign that you do care. But you can't let the situation consume you. Through understanding, emotional resilience, and compassion, it is possible to coexist with a pathological liar without losing sight of your own truth. While you may not always have control over their spiteful words, you do have control over how you will respond to them, and over the degree to which you let their words affect your emotional state.

Ch. 5: How to identify toxic behaviors within yourself

In the previous chapters, we described the various psychological and genetic factors that cause someone to resort to compulsive lying or exhibit *dark triad traits* — namely: narcissism, psychopathy, and Machiavellianism. It's possible that you spotted some facets of your own personality when perusing the symptoms of these disorders. Self-awareness is the first step toward personal development. Recognizing and addressing any unhealthy patterns in your own behavior may make it easier for you to navigate the fine line between normal personality quirks and harmful habits.

When my husband and I started dating, I was the happiest girl in the world. I couldn't believe what an incredible man he was. He was kind and compassionate, patient and understanding, intelligent and hardworking. I was so happy with him, and I loved imagining our future together. One morning, he called and said, "We need to talk." I knew those four words often came before a difficult conversation, but I couldn't imagine what was on his mind. When we finally sat down at lunch, he started by saying that he loved me but that he wasn't sure if things between us were going to work. "You criticize everything," he said.

At first, I was taken aback by his statement. I didn't see myself as a critical person. But as he shared specific instances when my words and actions had seemed overly negative, I began to see a pattern of behavior I hadn't recognized in myself before. It was a harsh reality check, but it was an important turning point for me. I realized that I had been displaying toxic behaviors without intending to. And that my words were damaging our relationship.

My critical nature is something I often excused as a mere byproduct of my quest for perfection. But this revelation forced me to confront some of the less flattering aspects of my personality. Coming to terms with these blemishes was difficult. But in doing so, I realized that, if I hadn't chosen to do it, I would have had to give up this amazing life I have now with my husband and kids.

Perhaps you're on a similar journey? Or perhaps you've begun to question the nature and efficacy of certain bad behaviors and habits you've picked up along the way. In any case, this chapter is intended to guide you along the path of self-discovery. We'll discuss how to identify personal toxic behaviors and how to transform them into healthier habits.

Remember, no one is perfect. We all have our weaknesses and shortcomings and things about ourselves that we'd like to improve. It's good to pursue continuous improvement. But our goal is not to become *perfect*. That's impossible. Instead, we understand that, though perfection is not attainable, there is great value in making a conscious effort to try to better ourselves each day.

Ten indicators of toxic behavior

In this section, we'll be looking at some "Do you...?" questions. These are questions that start with the phrase "Do you..." and then go on to describe a behavior or mindset that could potentially be toxic. The purpose of these questions is not to cast judgment but instead to help you reflect upon your own actions and attitudes. Remember, it's okay to answer "yes" to some of these questions. We all have our shortcomings. But if you find yourself answering "yes" repeatedly, then this could be an indication that some additional self-reflection and growth might be beneficial. Here are a few questions to consider:

Indicator 1. Do you use shaming language too often?

Sometimes we use phrases that belittle those around us, if only at a subconscious level. Additionally, we might use guilt as a means to manipulate others into doing our bidding. Shaming language can include statements like:

- "You should be ashamed of yourself!"
- "You're always messing things up!"
- "Why can't you be more like your older sister?"
- "Can't you do anything right?"
- "You're such a disappointment…"

Sound familiar?

The use of such shaming language can significantly harm the self-esteem and emotional wellbeing of those on the receiving end of such acerbic diatribes. This type of communication, which tends to be dismissive and belittling, could indicate a toxic behavior pattern.

Indicator 2. Do you tend to blame others for your problems?

Personal responsibility is an important skill to develop as an adult, but it's also a tough pill to swallow. It can be much easier to decide in our hearts that every struggle, problem, or challenge we face is because of someone else's actions. This is toxic behavior. If you struggle to apologize when you make a mistake or are convinced that you never really did anything wrong, then you're probably blaming others for your problems. Also, look out for sentences that start with the words, "Yes, but..." Such exclamations might look like this:

- Yes, but it wasn't my fault!
- Yes, but you made me do it!
- Yes, but you don't understand my situation!
- Yes, but you deserved it!
- Yes, but it wouldn't have happened if you hadn't said that!

These sentences are indicative of a person who is deflecting responsibility and quick to place the blame elsewhere. It is a harmful way of thinking, as it prevents you from recognizing your own potential role in the situation and inhibits personal growth.

Indicator 3. Do you try to one-up people who come to you with news?

I used to know a guy who always had a better (or worse) story than the one you just told.

- If you just won a million dollars in the lottery, he won three million a few years back.
- If you broke a leg during a weekend ski trip, he broke three legs on the mountain last year.

It was infuriating. If you feel the need to one-up people's stories, you're probably discouraging people from sharing things with you. It's hard to trust someone when you know that they're only listening to your story so that they can shove their own story in your ears.

Indicator 4. Do you take more than you give?

Relationships are a two-way street. We need to give as well as receive in order for them to work. If you are consistently taking more than you give—in the form of emotional support, time investment, or finances—then you may be cultivating an imbalanced and potentially toxic relationship dynamic.

- Do you frequently ask for favors but rarely offer help in return?
- Do you expect others to go out of their way for you, but aren't willing to do the same?
- Do you consume without reciprocating?

It's essential to foster a healthy balance of give-and-take in relationships, and any consistent imbalance could indicate a potentially harmful pattern.

Indicator 5. Do you say you don't like drama, but your life is full of it?

We all have that one friend or family member who is constantly lamenting the amount of drama in her life, but who refuses to believe that she is the impetus for at least half of it. Is this person you? Sometimes, we enjoy relishing the drama of everyday life more than we care to admit. If you frequently find yourself in the midst of conflict and arguments, then it might be time to ask yourself why.

Indicator 6. Do you gossip?

If you are frequently and cavalierly gossiping with your friends, family, or colleagues, then it probably won't be too long before they start to wonder how much discretion you are capable of. As we've learned, trust is crucial in relationships. Such actions may be perceived as toxic if they result in the spreading of rumors or confidential information without the consent of the parties involved. Gossip can sow discord, create confusion, and erode any expectation of trust that your familiars might have when considering maintaining a personal relationship with you.

Indicator 7. Do you fish for attention on social media?

If you've ever created a social media post that said something like:

OMG! Why do people hate me so much!? #SoHurt #Struggling

Then you might be guilty of engaging in attention-seeking behavior. While it's fine to share your feelings and experiences online, consistently posting vague, emotionally-charged statements to incite worry or curiosity among your friends could be seen as manipulative and toxic.

Indicator 8. Do you complain a lot?

Life is hard. And there are days when we can't help but complain about everything that's happening. That's normal. But it's not normal if every conversation you have revolves around your grievances. Chronic complaining not only creates a negative atmosphere, it also pushes people away. If you are constantly focusing on the *negative* and disregarding the many *positive* aspects of life, then this could be indicative of a toxic behavior that needs addressing.

Indicator 9. Do you try to dominate every conversation?

There are many reasons why someone might attempt to dominate a conversation. It could simply be due to enthusiasm about the topic being discussed, or it could be due to nerves. Like many other items on this list, if the behavior rarely happens, then it's not a problem. I know I like to dominate conversations when the topic of films comes up. (I really love films.) However, my constant interjections can become an issue if I don't monitor my enthusiasm.

Dominating a conversation doesn't always take the form of a constant patter. It might arise in the form of rude or inappropriate jokes that cut through the milieu of enjoyable banter. If such behavior persists, people will get the sense that we don't care about what they have to say. They'll walk away with the impression that we only care about ourselves and our preconceived notions. If we don't keep a handle on these overbearing tendencies, we'll have no one to chat with.

Indicator 10. Are your friends disappearing?

It can be incredibly demoralizing to watch friendship after friendship fail. If you've noticed that your friend group is dissipating, it might be a sign that your own toxic behaviors are playing a role in driving people away. It is natural for friendships to shift and change over time. But a rapid loss of interpersonal relationships may indicate that your actions or your attitude are negatively impacting those around you. This could be due to many reasons. However, if after ruminating on your predicament, you still cannot identify the source of your assumed social faux pas, then it may be worth seeking out the advice of a trusted family member or therapist. They can provide you with an objective lens that should help to guide you through the process of self-reflection, thus helping you identify and address any potential toxic behaviors.

How to stop being toxic

Harmonizing the divergent whispers that emanate from the light and dark angels that reside atop each shoulder is a lifelong quest. We should all strive to cultivate habits that bring out our best selves while mitigating those that strain our relationships. Becoming cognizant of the moments at which we engage in malevolent or toxic behavior is the first step to making positive changes in our lives. From such a vantage point, we can begin to understand the root causes of our negative patterns, develop strategies to counteract them and foster more constructive, empathetic, and respectful relationships. In this section, we'll discuss several tips that should help to reduce toxicity and promote positive personal growth in your life.

Tip 1. Identify your own insecurities

Much of our toxic behavior is rooted in insecurity. This insecurity makes us feel a variety of emotions, like fear, jealousy, anger, and shame. Recall the tale of my first bully, Freddy. He became the playground bully because of how vulnerable he felt in his broken home. His inability to control the chaotic devastation caused by his parents' divorce prompted him to attempt to assert control over something more manageable, like the smaller kids on the playground. We've all felt prone to engage in destructive behavior after experiencing similar bouts of insecurity.

- Perhaps the financial struggles that your family went through when you were young have prompted you to be hyper-controlling when it comes to your finances.
- Perhaps a domineering parent never afforded you any privacy, and so you tend to keep to yourself, remaining secretive and distant, even when an opportunity for intimacy is called for.
- Perhaps a series of failed relationships has led you to become overly possessive or suspicious of your current partner.
- Perhaps losing out on a significant career opportunity has bred a sense of bitterness and resentment, which sometimes spills out onto your colleagues.
- Perhaps the feeling of always being compared to a more successful sibling has fostered an intense need to prove your worth, even at the expense of your health and relationships.

Whatever the root of your insecurity might be, it is important to understand that discovering the impetus of your pain does not give you carte blanche to continue perpetuating toxic behavior. While it may provide context and a better understanding of why you behave in certain ways, it is not an excuse to keep hurting those around you. Even if someone else is the cause of your insecurities, you are still the executive of your own actions. There is great power in discovering the fount from which your insecurities emanate. Once you do, you will finally know your enemy for who he truly is, and your efforts can be directed more appropriately.

- You'll no longer be trying to merely shout less. Instead, you'll be trying to overcome your fear of being ignored.
- You'll no longer be trying to stop lying. Instead, you'll be trying to defeat your fear of being rejected for how you feel.
- You'll no longer be trying to stop complaining. Instead, you'll be trying to break the habit of assuming the worst about your reality.

Dealing with personal toxicity is like dealing with weeds. To rid your garden of them completely, you have to get to the root. The same applies to your toxic traits. By addressing the root cause as well as the resultant behaviors that these causes manifest, we hope to encourage a holistic healing process, one that focuses on our mental and emotional development. It is only by engaging in honest bouts of self-reflection that we can hope to grow beyond our current limitations and blossom into the person we aspire to be.

Tip 2. "Seek first to understand, then to be understood."

In Stephen Covey's influential 1989 bestselling book "The 7 Habits of Highly Effective People," Covey offers this tidbit of sage advice:

Seek first to understand, then to be understood.

This short sentence goes a long way in describing how we might become more effective listeners. Sometimes, the best thing you can do to curtail your own toxic behavior is to simply practice talking less and listening more. By doing so, you're accomplishing two important things:

- First, you're showing the other party that you're interested in what they have to say and that you care about their story.
- Second, you're giving yourself an opportunity to truly grasp their perspective and empathize with their feelings or concerns.

By easing up on your ego and allowing the other person more space to converse, we hope to engender more productive conversations, minimize misunderstanding, and, ultimately, reduce the tension in our interactions. Such habits can also help us to avoid making assumptions or jumping to conclusions, which might lead to unnecessary conflict.

Tip 3. Understand the difference between "reacting" and "responding."

Before you allow someone else's words or actions to send you into a triggered state, take a breath and remind yourself to remain calm during the discourse. Then, think about the particulars of the interaction. Ask yourself:

- What is causing the other party to act this way?
- Why are you allowing them to influence your peace of mind?
- Are you dealing with a reasonable person, or someone who just wants to convey their rage?

Our aim here is to emphasize the difference between "reacting and responding." When someone is in a *reactive mode*, they might be prone to blurt out a toxic retort, as if their utterance was a mere *Pavlovian response*—the result of a volcanic blast of emotion rather than rational rumination. A wise response entails taking a moment to understand the situation, internalizing the content of the discourse, and then expressing your thoughts in a respectful and constructive manner. Obviously, the chaotic exigencies of life do not always allow for such sober moments of reflection. However, the ability to maintain your composure during such heated exchanges will help to prevent the interaction from devolving into a toxic shouting match.

Tip 4. Make a conscious effort to empathize

If you're used to dominating the conversation, then this tip might require a fair amount of effort to pull off. When talking to a friend, listen carefully to what they're saying and attempt to understand their emotions and experiences at a deep and emphatic level. This means letting go of your need to "win the argument," instead focusing on connecting with the other person in a humane way. By showing compassion and empathy during such encounters, we're creating a safe space for open dialogue and mutual respect, thus fostering healthier and more fulfilling relationships.

Tip 5. Don't be afraid to be vulnerable to those you trust

If you've ever watched an abused rescue dog interact with its new owner, you'll notice how it is unwilling to rollover and reveal its tender belly. If you have sustained traumatic emotional injuries in the past, then it is natural for the mind to be wary of potential threats, even from those who mean us no harm. Once a relationship has progressed enough such that moments of intimacy and vulnerability are called for, it is common for traumatized individuals to refuse to give up their defensive posture. But it's important to understand that vulnerability is not always a sign of weakness. Instead, such intimate encounters allow us to connect with another person on a deeper level. Letting down your guard with trusted friends or family can help to heal old wounds and change toxic patterns of behavior. Don't be afraid to share your fears and insecurities with those who genuinely care about your wellbeing. In doing so, you invite others to empathize with you, to offer support, and to share their own vulnerabilities, thereby strengthening your relationship and allowing the creation of a conduit through which understanding, compassion, and mutual respect can flow.

Tip 6. Admit when you're wrong

We all hate to admit when we're wrong. Admitting a mistake can feel as if we're demonstrating weakness or incompetence. But in truth, taking ownership of one's actions is a sign of maturity. It shows that you value truth and fairness above your ego. When we acknowledge our missteps, we not only demonstrate accountability, but we also foster a dialogue of honesty and openness with those around us. If you've let your toxic behaviors lead you astray, acknowledging your faults is a vital step toward making amends and breaking the cycle. Remember, it's okay to be wrong. But it's not ok to refuse to learn and grow from these moments.

Tip 7. Ask for help

As we have emphasized many times throughout this book, don't be afraid to ask for help if you feel that your toxic behaviors are deleterious to your life goals, or to the welfare of your friends and family. There's no shame in seeking professional assistance from therapists or counselors who are trained to help you make sense of your emotions and construct strategies for instigating real change in your behaviors. Support groups can also be helpful as they allow you to connect with individuals who are facing similar life challenges. Sharing your experiences with others who are walking a similar path can be illuminating and empowering.

Remember, the quest to maximize your physical and psychological health is a venture that has no endpoint. Be patient with yourself, be honest about your limitations, and try not to dwell on your own personal shortcomings. By making a pledge to recognize and understand the nature of our behaviors, we aim to become more compassionate, mindful, and balanced individuals. This is a noble endeavor. And it is the path that every wise and humane person should walk.

Ch. 6: Strategies for handling bullies in the workplace

The press releases of companies and corporations are often quick to proclaim, "Our people are our most important product." But, as anyone who has walked an office floor knows, sometimes your coworkers can be a real pain in the backside. As employees in a modern office, we are obliged to work with a diverse range of individuals, each with their unique idiosyncrasies and off-putting quirks. Navigating such relationships can be a daunting task, especially when these behaviors veer into the toxic territory of *bullying*.

Managing bullying behavior in a workplace can be particularly challenging because the offending party is often quick to insist that he or she is operating under the guise of mere "assertiveness" or "competitiveness." But toxic workplace behaviors—like public humiliation, undue criticism, or social exclusion—can create a hostile work environment that imposes an additional burden on each employee. Hence, it is essential that employees appreciate the importance of actively counteracting such behaviors to ensure a healthy and respectful workplace for all.

In their 2017 National Survey, *The Workplace Bullying and Trauma Institute (WBTI)* defined workplace bullying as:

Repeated mistreatment of an employee by one or more employees; abusive conduct that is: threatening, humiliating, or intimidating, work sabotage, or verbal abuse.

In surmising their research, WBTI found that:

- 19% of Americans report being bullied, and another 19% have witnessed it at work.
- 61% of Americans are aware that abusive conduct has taken place in their workplace.
- 29% of bully victims choose to remain silent about their experience.
- And, 60% of workplace bullies are identified as being "the boss."

The WBTI survey estimated that 60 million Americans are affected by workplace bullying each year. If this is the case, then clearly workplace bullying is an issue that requires some attention.

In this chapter, we will explore various strategies to handle workplace bullies, and discuss some tactics that you might utilize to safeguard your emotional wellness while still managing to remain productive and cultivate a positive work environment. Each section will offer guidance on recognizing the signs and symptoms of workplace bullying and should help equip you to address such workplace challenges.

How to spot a workplace bully

If you are to successfully manage your workplace interactions, then understanding the unique eccentricities of each one of your toxic coworkers should provide you with a roadmap to navigate such challenging workplace dynamics. What follows is not an exhaustive psychological treatise on Jungian personality types. Instead, we'll briefly list a basic inventory of workplace characters that you're probably already quite familiar with. Hopefully, this taxonomy will provide us with some insight into the *modus operandi* of such personas, and prepare you to be ready for their offenses when they occur.

Toxic Coworker Type 1: The Diva

The Diva has an unhealthy sense of entitlement. She wants to be fawned over and pampered. And heaven forbid she gets her hands (or her gown) dirty. The Diva can often be found delegating her work to others and shirking her responsibilities, all while craving the spotlight when praise is being doled out following the completion of a group project. A Diva may be prone to a subtle sort of bullying behavior—perhaps never resorting to yelling or profanity, but instead utilizing manipulation and dramatics to pursue her goals.

Toxic Coworker Type 2: The Know-it-All

No one knows it all. But this fact does not deter your resident Know-it-All from offering a solution about the best way to approach every office task. Unfortunately, when the Know-it-All insists that things be done a certain way, his or her constant interjections might discourage others from expressing their ideas or exploring different strategies. Additionally, Know-it-Alls might often discount or discredit the input of others. Or they might insist that any course of action that does not involve their input is an unwise action and can only result in inferior results. This type of bullying, while less severe than other forms, can be equally detrimental to workplace harmony.

Toxic Coworker Type 3: The Critic

The constant Critic will take any opportunity to undermine and belittle your efforts. Nothing you do is ever good enough. And even your most heroic accomplishments are met with scrutiny and disdain. For deep-seated psychological reasons, the Critic needs to see faults in others. They may hide behind the guise of "constructive criticism," but their feedback rarely provides any valuable insights for growth. Instead, it only serves to bolster their own ego. The Critic's bullying tactics might not come in the form of a flying fist. But, if let to foster, such behavior can erode the morale and productivity of the workforce.

Toxic Coworker Type 4: The Gatekeeper

The Gatekeeper holds the keys to the kingdom. This kingdom might be a project committee seat, an office resource, an opportunity for promotion, or even the hallway that leads to the boss's office itself. Gatekeepers can be challenging to deal with because they like to use the leverage of their strategic position to prevent coworkers from advancing along in their career goals. Their bullying behavior may even delve into the social realm, where they utilize subterfuge to monitor employee fraternizing and control the social dynamics of the workplace. This might include intentionally leaving certain colleagues off an invite list, or excluding them from office gatherings and important meetings. By perpetuating a culture of favoritism, the Gatekeeper's toxic influence can affect the entire office, resulting in a stifling work environment that hinders collaboration and mutual support.

Toxic Coworker Type 5: The Backstabber

The Backstabber archetype describes the guy who is willing to stab you in the back if doing so might result in advancement for himself. Backstabbers might initially appear amicable and trustworthy. But they are forever plotting behind the scenes, waiting for an opportunity to capitalize upon your vulnerabilities. The Backstabber might befriend you with the sole intent of learning your strengths and weaknesses. When your weaknesses are identified, he might exploit them by spreading rumors, taking credit for your work, or undermining your efforts in front of your superiors.

Toxic Coworker Type 6: The Tyrant

The Tyrant is the most common type of bully that you will find on the office floor. His behavior is particularly stressing because The Tyrant usually has authority over you. In other words, he's your boss. Recall that the above-cited WBTI study found that 60% of reported workplace bullying originated from the boss himself. The boss Tyrant will use his title to justify his behavior. His bullying behaviors can manifest in the form of belittling subordinates, setting unrealistic expectations, and fostering a work environment fueled by fear. This form of bullying can be particularly damaging as it not only impacts your professional life but also undermines your self-confidence and worth. The Tyrant can be subtly manipulative or overtly hostile, but their desire to control and intimidate extends beyond their mere thirst for profit. True Tyrants aren't just trying to get the best out of their team. Instead, they enjoy the act of bullying more than they enjoy any spoils that might be garnered from their whip-cracking ways. Your office floor can quickly devolve into an unbearable pit of quarrels if it is under the rule of a Tyrant. His behaviors are typically quick to result in a high staff turnover rate, low morale, and poor team performance.

How to confront a workplace bully

Now that we've enumerated six of the types of bullies you are likely to encounter in the workplace, let's discuss the process by which you might go about rectifying the situation. The first move you make should *not* be to march down to the Human Resources office. (That might come later.) But it is usually worth taking a moment to try to have a heart-to-heart discussion with your toxic coworker if possible. These are the steps you might take:

Step 1. Decide which bullying behaviors must stop

Before your encounter, decide about the types of behavior that you will and will not tolerate from your bully. Human banter and spirited discourse almost necessarily involves multiple parties making witty remarks and caustic retorts. Additionally, the productive output of each employee in the workplace must be critiqued and criticized to some extent. If it wasn't, then we would never improve. So, it's typically not wise to approach this meeting with the intent of setting a boundary in the form of:

- "You can never make jokes about me again."
- "You must never criticize my work again."
- "You must never come near me again."

Such demands would not be possible to fulfill in most office environments. Instead, have a play to provide your bully with a specific type of discourse that you will not allow. Make sure you are clear about exactly where you want to draw the line.

Step 2. Make a private appointment with your bully

Once you've mapped out the boundaries you wish to draw, it's time to sit down with your bully. Don't try to corner them in the hallway or catch them in front of a group of coworkers. Instead, organize to meet in a calm and neutral location, like a corner office or a local coffee shop. Our goal is to create a safe space where you and the bully both feel comfortable. The calmer they are, the more likely they will be to have an adult conversation without resorting to their typical bullying behavior to cope with the confrontation.

Step 3. Describe the behaviors that have prompted this meeting

Once you sit down for your one-on-one, calmly recount the examples of bullying behavior that have prompted you to initiate this meeting. Describe the behavior succinctly. But don't go into extreme detail, and don't come at him with a list of grievances that require more than five minutes to describe. Instead, calmly define the specific actions that have caused you to experience anxiety.

Step 4. Explain the impact that this behavior has had on you

Once you've described what the bully has done, explain how it has affected you. This is the part where you must try to get the bully to see the impact of their actions. If you're dealing with a rational and good-natured human being, then this interaction might just mark the moment at which all of his toxic behaviors cease forever. Often, we are not the victim of bullying because the bully holds a negative opinion of us. Instead, it may be the case that the bully is merely reflecting his opinion of himself. Hearing how his actions have made you feel can be just the thing to get him to realize the undesirable ramifications of his ploys.

Step 5. Conclude by reiterating which behaviors are to stop now

Now that you have described the problem try to conclude the meeting in the same way you would conclude a business negotiation. Ensure that both parties understand how they are to proceed in the future, and shake hands to affirm your newfound commitment. Doing so will aid in establishing a clear and mutual understanding that certain behaviors will not be tolerated moving forward. Reiterate the specific behaviors that must cease, making sure that there's no ambiguity in the bully's mind. Ask the bully to confirm their understanding of the malevolent nature of the behaviors. And make sure he knows that the point of this conversation has not been to instigate a personal attack. Instead, it was a necessary step to maintain the integrity of the professional relationship. Remember, your main objective is not to change the bully as a person but to address the bullying behavior. It may not guarantee an immediate change, but it sets the stage for improvement and can be the catalyst for change.

Step 6. Apply your new rules consistently

As anyone who has ever tried to stick to a new weight loss regimen can attest to, the pillar of rules that we so confidently set in place on Day 1 of our diet are often forgotten on Day 2. Hence, even if you were able to accrue a heartfelt commitment from your bully in the previous steps, don't be surprised if you spot him reverting back to his hold ways as the workweek progresses. It is common for a bully to back off for a while and then to make little comments in an effort to re-test the waters. Subconsciously, he might be trying to see which of your newly erected boundaries are made of stone and which ones are made of glass. If you eventually come to discover that your bully has fully and completely reverted back to his old ways, then it is clear that a heart-to-heart conversation is not going to be the antidote to your anguish. In the next section, we'll discuss how you might proceed following such an undesirable outcome.

What to do if the bullying persists

If attempts to solve your bullying woes via direct conversation fail, then what recourse do you have in the workplace? Answering this question would depend upon the specific arrangement that you have with your employer, and the title of the person doing the bullying. If the malevolent behavior is coming from the boss himself, then your options might be limited. In any case, let's examine a few tips that should help to put you in a better position to act decisively.

Tip 1: Try to discuss your feelings with your bully once more

As a last-ditch effort, you might try repeating the steps described in the previous section. Sit down with your bully one last time and try to convey your feelings to him. Be warned that if the first confrontation didn't work, then the second confrontation probably won't go very well. But if you feel as if you have made some progress since the last encounter, then one more encounter might bear some fruit.

Tip 2: Document the abuse

Keep a journal of when and where each bullying incident took place. Write down what happened, who witnessed it, and how you responded during the altercation. Make a copy of any emails or memos that might give weight to your claims. And if the bully is likely to assert that your work performance has been poor, be sure to collect any reports that might serve as evidence to the contrary.

Tip 2: Do your research

Not all companies have policies that prevent workplace bullying. But it's worth looking through the employee handbook to see if such a doctrine exists. If there is a policy prohibiting the behavior you're experiencing, then you might be able to use this information to your advantage if you intend to file a formal complaint.

Tip 3: Talk to Human Resources (HR)

As you might have noticed, this entire chapter has been devoted to addressing your bullying issue *without* including any outside parties. Often, mature coworkers can resolve such tensions themselves with tact and discretion. However, the Human Resources office exists for a reason. If you have to march down to HR, make sure you are ready to clearly explain the conflict in a logical and emotionless manner. Bring all your documentation with you so that you have something to back up your claims. It might even be worth your while to calculate the degree of lost productivity hours that you think your brutish coworker is costing you and the company. In other words, make it known that the problem is not just a matter of hurt feelings but an assault on the company's bottom line. Make it clear that the situation isn't just causing personal distress, but also undermining team morale, productivity, and the harmonious working environment as a whole. In demonstrating the wider implications of the bully's actions, you'll emphasize that it is an issue that warrants HR's attention and not just a personal conflict. Additionally, you might consider talking to an employment attorney if your situation is particularly complex and stressful. They'll be able to provide you with a clearer picture of your options.

Tip 4: Find a new job.

Once you have exhausted all of your in-house options, then only one alternative remains: *quit*. Such a retreat might be your only viable course of action, particularly if:

- The bullying continues despite your efforts.
- The organizational culture can't be bothered to address the matter.
- Your work performance is negatively affected, and you find yourself unable to focus.
- Other employment opportunities are readily available.
- It's the boss himself that is doing the bullying.

No job is worth sacrificing your mental health for. Even if quitting your present line of work results in some transient financial agitations, you will probably not regret it if the position you land in is free of such stressful encounters or toxic coworkers. In the long run, you'll be better off if you can find a supportive work environment that respects and values each employee. Leaving a toxic workplace can open up new opportunities and pathways in your career that might better align with your personal values and ambitions.

Ch. 7: Strategies for handling toxic family members

In previous chapters, we discussed the prevalence of toxic behaviors in our academic, romantic, and work-related interactions. But home is where the heart is. Surely our bullying woes cannot transcend the threshold of our houses, right?

Well, as anyone who has ever interacted with an alcoholic father or a mordant mother-in-law knows, familial relations can sometimes be the most challenging relations of all. The social dynamics of our families are complex, and the roots of these relationships grow deep, making them difficult to manage, mitigate, or (when necessary) to break. The ones with whom we have spent our most formative years have the power to impact our emotional wellbeing at a level that is not possible for strangers or new acquaintances. While our homes should provide us with a safe and nurturing environment, the sad reality is that, for many people, familial arrangements are a great source of stress and hostility.

Like so many married women, I have a mother-in-law story. Things were always a little tense between us. And I had hoped that, after the wedding cake had been cut, she would lighten up a bit and accept me into the family. Oh, how wrong I was...

As soon as the honeymoon ended, I felt as if my mother-in-law had made it her mission in life to push my buttons and cross every red line I could possibly draw.

- She would constantly manipulate my husband to get her way, and had no respect for my role as his wife.
- She consistently disregarded my parenting decisions, undermining my authority and causing discord among my children.
- She treated our home as if it was her own, showing up unannounced and overstepping her role as a grandmother.
- Even in public, she would make critical or derogatory comments about me or my children.

My husband and I had started fighting more and more because of all the pressure we were under. I felt he wasn't being supportive of me, and he felt stuck in the middle of the two people he cared about most. It got so bad that I was regularly calling realtors in an attempt to evaluate our housing options in another state. For a while, I thought that the only way I was going to save my marriage would be to put some distance between me and my mother-in-law.

Thankfully, I eventually realized that this was not a viable solution. After all, I wouldn't have been the least bit surprised if she managed to convince my husband to take her along with us. In those days, she'd never let me "steal her little boy" after all. Things had to change. Because now my marriage was officially on the line.

The short version is this: my mother-in-law and I eventually managed to sort things out. And although I would not have believed it if you had told me this in the first year of our marriage, today we're thick as thieves. It definitely wasn't easy. It took a journey of multiple conversations over multiple months. A lot of tears (and even more cake) were involved. But we eventually came to understand and trust each other.

Just like I almost tried to run away from my familial problems, you too might be considering a similar course of action. Unfortunately, it is true that *estrangement* might be your only viable option. Sometimes the best way to rectify a situation is to disengage from it. But before you start packing your bags, let's take a moment to consider a few other options. In this chapter, we'll discuss some tools that you might find beneficial in managing such challenging family dynamics. These strategies should help to promote open communication, assertiveness, and compassion, thus enabling you to interact more effectively with your family members and transform your toxic environment into a more nurturing and supportive one.

Toxic vs. Difficult Family Members

Before we discuss how to deal with a toxic family member, we need to first figure out if the bane of your existence is a genuinely *toxic* person or just a *difficult* one. Almost all human relationships can be *difficult* at one time or another. But this doesn't make them *toxic*. Part of being a mature adult is learning to cope with the spectrum of eccentricities that each of our friends and family members are prone to manifest. Indeed, this enterprise is not necessarily altruistic. Just as you find their modes of behavior to be taxing, they often feel the exact same way about you. We're all human after all. We all come packaged with a consortium of quirks and quackery that synergize to craft the unique and interesting persona that we present to the world. Of course, some personas can be more toxic than others. How are we to know when the line has been crossed?

The clinical psychologist Dr. Perpetua Neo provides us with this definition of toxicity:

A toxic person is someone who regularly displays actions and behaviors that hurt others or otherwise negatively impact the lives of the people around them...

If the relationship in question results in physical or sexual abuse, then you should extract yourself from the environment immediately and seek professional help. However, if the agitation is more subtle, and you're still attempting to classify the degree of injury that is taking place, the following indicators might serve as useful guideposts.

Indicator 1: Your anxieties peak when they're around

If the thought of spending another evening in proximity to a certain family member causes you to feel anxiety or stress, then this might be an indication that something is not right in your relationship. Some people seem to have a unique ability to suck all the joy out of a room. Their mere presence can leave us feeling drained, agitated, and reaching for our headache medicine. If someone in your family is a source of constant criticism, disrespect, or incessant negativity, then you may be dealing with a toxic stressor in your life.

Indicator 2: They have an acerbic tongue

It's natural to disagree and hold differing opinions. But such conversations can become toxic if your interlocuter insists on dismissing your feelings, opinions, or experiences. Nobody deserves to be belittled all the time. If they downplay your achievements, mock your ambitions, or invalidate your emotions, then such behaviors need not be tolerated.

Indicator 3: They violate your boundaries

Recall from my earlier story how my mother-in-law was the queen of violating our personal space. Or, as my husband and I used to call her, she was a "habitual line stepper" — a phrase we borrowed from Charlie Murphy's appearance on the original *Dave Chappelle Show*. A *habitual line stepper* is someone who persistently encroaches upon or is indifferent to your personal boundaries. This can range from disregarding your privacy, to breaking your house rules, to being verbally abusive.

Healthy relationships are built on mutual respect and trust. This includes fostering respect for boundaries and the sanctity of the family home. If a family member regularly invades this space and disregards your requests to do otherwise, then this behavior is of the toxic variety.

Indicator 4: They manipulate you into doing their bidding

Toxic family members use many tactics to pursue their personal goals. They might use an overt form of manipulation like physical force, or (more commonly) they use coercion to coax you into complying with their wishes. This can manifest in many forms:

- emotional blackmail,
- guilt-tripping,
- citing your many insecurities,
- appealing to your sense of obligation,

- noting that you are in debt to them (financially, emotionally, or otherwise),
- or, by exploiting your empathy and kindness by playing the victim card.

Despite the tactics they might employ, the end goal is the same—to get you to act in a way that serves their interests, often at your expense.

Indicator 5: Their reactions are unnecessarily harsh

Harsh censure can take many forms. It could look like a parent grounding a child for several months because they "only" got an A on their exam and not an A+. Or, it could look like an auntie spouting a persistent stream of passive-aggressive comments just because she had twenty minutes to kill before her bus arrived. For me, it was my mother-in-law claiming that I was trying to sabotage her relationship with her son and ruin my child's academic career.

Toxic people like to make it look like they're playing by the rules, even though they're really making the rules up as they go. Their reaction to the smallest annoyance far exceeds the severity of the offense. Their displays of histrionics are a tactic they utilize to keep you on your toes—forever anxious and always seeking to appease them. Such a manipulation of familial power dynamics is a major red flag, and an indicator of a potentially toxic individual.

Indicator 6: They're predictably unpredictable

Some toxic people have a hair-trigger—frequently set off by the smallest slight and prone to outbursts that would put a screaming toddler to shame. The most innocuous action can be perceived as an act of disrespect or aggression. Such people are often quick to give you an earful of their emotions. But less willing to tell you exactly what you did wrong. (They may not even know themselves…) But by stirring the spirits of confusion, they can maintain their power and keep you from being able to do anything about it. If you feel like you always have to "walk on eggshells" around a particular familial acquaintance, then it is likely that they fall into the toxic category.

How to cope with a toxic family member

In glancing at our above list, it's likely that a few individuals in your life may have come to mind. If you keep an eye out for these signs, plus the additional indicators discussed in previous chapters, then you should be well on your way to spotting any proximate bullying behavior in your own life and in the lives of those closest to you. Note that we should never be quick to judge someone. It's never wise to make snap judgments about people before you've had an opportunity to observe their behavior over time and understand their motives. However, if a pattern of toxicity becomes evident, it's essential to take steps to protect the wellbeing of yourself and those around you.

Managing the behavior of a spiteful family member can be tricky because their behavior might be propped up and supported by multiple members of your family tree. Often, citing an issue with one branch of this tree necessarily entails agitating each of the surrounding branches as well. For example, my relationship with my husband became strained even though my problem wasn't with him, it was with his mother. The ties that bind families together are tangled and complex. Disentangling the web of toxicity that rots within the coiled roots can be a challenging one. But with the right tools, it can be done. The key lies in understanding that you cannot immediately change their behavior or mode of living. But you *can* control where these interactions take place and how you respond to them. Here are some strategies to get you started.

Tip 1: Create a solid family support system

If you are to have a confrontation with a particular toxic family member, then you need to present a united front. For a reason why, look no farther than the bible:

- In Mark 3:25, Jesus states, "if a house be divided against itself, that house cannot stand."
- In Matthew 12:25, Jesus states, "Every kingdom divided against itself is brought to desolation; and every city or house divided against itself shall not stand."
- In Luke 11:17 Jesus states, "Any kingdom divided against itself will be ruined, and a house divided against itself will fall."

Obviously, if the *powers on high* thought it necessary to repeat this expression three times, then we would be wise to take note of it. The point being, it will be quite difficult to confront a toxic family member if the other members of the family do not support your claims. Unfortunately, it is often the case that ancillary family members would rather stay out of the conflict, insistent either that it's not happening or that it's not their problem to address. Such an avoidance strategy can complicate the situation, making it feel like you're fighting a battle on multiple fronts.

If your family members are initially reluctant to validate your claims, try to emphasize that your intent is not to gang up on the toxic person. Instead, your aim should be to build a network of understanding and solidarity such that you can call upon more allies to help mediate the discourse should the toxic behaviors persist. Remember, confronting a toxic family member is not just about asserting your rights; it's about promoting healthier relationships for everyone in the family.

Tip 2: Sit down with your bully and discuss your boundaries

Recall in the previous chapter when we described a six-step plan for confronting your workplace bully. The steps were as follows:

1. Decide which bullying behaviors must stop.
2. Make a private appointment with your bully.
3. Describe the behaviors that have prompted this meeting.
4. Explain the impact that this behavior has had on you.
5. Conclude by reiterating which behaviors are to stop now.
6. Apply your new rules consistently.

You can turn back and review these steps at your leisure. Our aim here is to emphasize that a similar process of boundary-building can be utilized during a heart-to-heart conversation with a hostile family member. Our goals are the same. We want to clearly and assertively communicate our feelings and set up a boundary in which the toxic behaviors must not persist. Make it clear how the behaviors you're experiencing are negatively affecting you, and let them know, in no uncertain terms, that consequences will follow if things don't change. Such consequences might come in the form of limiting contact, supervised visits, or even complete estrangement if things get particularly toxic. Though difficult, it's essential to ensure that these consequences are not mere empty threats but definite measures that you are prepared to follow through on.

Tip 3: Don't engage in their games

In his book "Games People Play," the psychiatrist Eric Berne attempted to illuminate the hidden social dynamics that are at play in our daily interactions. He contended that many of our encounters could be understood in terms of psychological "games" — i.e., recurring patterns of behavior that people engage in subconsciously, playing a role within a defined script of expected reactions and outcomes. These games are driven by our hidden needs or desires, such as the need for attention and validation.

For example, in the game termed "Wooden Leg," a practitioner uses his perceived weakness (i.e., his "wooden leg") as an excuse for calling on others to do his bidding. If your kid brother always insisted on riding in the front seat because he felt perpetually carsick, or if your auntie would insist that you must pick up her groceries because of her lower back pain, then you have probably been a victim of the game *Wooden Leg*.

"Games People Play" was a financial success shortly after it was launched in 1964, making it one of the first *pop psych* books ever published. Though it lacks academic rigor, it nonetheless serves as a unique template for describing human behavior.

People like to play games. And (as you're probably well aware) toxic family members like to play a *lot* of games. Mother-in-laws are known for having quite a few cards up their sleeves. They might:

- Fame illness to garner more attention from their son.
- Cite their age as a reason for avoiding familial commitments.
- Manipulate your feelings by using guilt or obligation to get their way.

Eric Berne filled an entire book with such games. Your approach doesn't need to be so thorough. But, when interacting with a spiteful family member, try to remain cognizant of the patterns they employ to pursue their goals. Toxic people are often very good at manipulating others, and mind games are their forte. They will inevitably try and find a way to violate the boundaries that you erected in the pervious step. But stick to your guns. Don't let them derail you from your path. When a toxic person realizes that their games are no longer effective, they might decide to reevaluate their own behavior. This is how epiphanies are achieved, and relationships are salvaged.

Tip 4: Enforce the consequences

At this point, you've established your familial support system, communicated your goals, and laid down your boundaries. Now, the ball is in their court. If the bully in your life still insists on encroaching on your territory, then you must be willing to enforce the consequences that you laid out in the initial conversation. If you don't, then this entire process was in vain.

I know that enforcing consequences is difficult. I was terrified when I had to tell my mother-in-law that we would not be coming to Thanksgiving dinner because of how she'd been acting. I had warned her multiple times, as had my husband. In all honesty, we probably should have given her fewer warnings. Eventually, we had to make the call if we wanted things to change. Of course, it caused a huge upset, and I was painted as the biggest villain in the world. But the important part was that I stood up for myself, and my husband was on board. By sticking to our guns, we showed a united front and communicated our message clearly: "Our boundaries must not be crossed."

When to resort to estrangement

Not all relationships can be salvaged.

Not all bullies wish to change their ways.

Sometimes, toxic family members leave us no choice but to limit (or completely cut off) our involvement with them. This is a decision that should not be taken lightly. The impact of such a choice is widespread and long-lasting. In the end, coping with a toxic family member is a long road of self-awareness. And we must walk down this road while knowing that it doesn't always lead to greener pastures. If you have exhausted all your other options, then it may be time to cut ties completely. This is what we'll discuss in the next chapter.

Ch. 8: When is it time to walk away?

I have a cousin named Andrew. We were close growing up, and out of all my extended family, I probably liked Andrew the most. Unfortunately, Andrew got married to a toxic woman named Alice. Our entire family disliked her. We all knew Andrew had made a bad decision. And some family members even boycotted their wedding. This profoundly impacted Andrew as he felt unsupported, unloved, and rejected by the people most important to him.

Alice was a troubled person. In retrospect, I can see now that she needed therapy much more than she needed a whirlwind romance with my cousin. She was blatantly manipulative, lied constantly, and was not afraid to resort to histrionics if she felt someone had committed an offensive act toward her. The signs of toxicity were all there. But Andrew truly loved her. And, as the saying goes, love is blind.

As the years progressed, we saw Andrew less and less. And then, one day, there was a knock at our door. I opened it to find Andrew there with a suitcase and a nasty cut on his cheek. I was surprised when I saw him, but even more shocked when I learned that he had decided to leave Alice. She'd finally pushed him over the edge and threw a vase at him, resulting in a cut that needed twelve stitches. The fact that it was so close to his left eye seemed to have finally scared him into taking a second look at his relationship. He'd had enough, and although she cried and screamed and begged him to stay, he knew it was time to pack his bags and leave for good.

I was so grateful that he'd come to our home. We made space in the spare bedroom, and it felt a little like old times for the week that he stayed. There were moments when I could see him coming to terms with the weight of his new reality. He'd go quiet for a few minutes before reappearing in the world with a forced smile and red eyes. I could tell he still loved her.

If you've ever witnessed someone emerge from a toxic relationship, or if you've fled one yourself, then you'll know what I'm talking about. Sometimes, no matter how much we want things to be different, we have to accept the fact that things are not going to work out. Sometimes our only option is to walk away.

- But how do we know when to walk out that front door?
- How do we disentangle ourselves from a person who has been so dear to us for so long?
- And how do we go on without them?

These are the questions we'll be discussing in this chapter.

How to know when to walk away

Sometimes, when we have become settled in a lengthy relationship, it becomes difficult to see the forest for the trees. This is especially true in toxic relationships where manipulation, gaslighting, or microaggressions can make us second-guess our instincts. Often, we become so entangled with the daily affairs of life that we fail to see the larger pattern of negativity that looms above the everyday chaos. In this section, we've listed several questions to ponder if you are attempting to navigate the miasma of doubt that we all feel when we're considering drafting an exit strategy for a doomed relationship.

Question 1: Have you been confusing hope with denial?

I personally think my cousin Andrew should never have married Alice. (Although I did indeed go to their wedding—mostly because they had free cake). However, as even he would admit now, the warning signs were always there. But he held out hope that things would get better.

Hope is a sticky thing. Hope will keep you glued to places that you should no longer reside in. Hope will try to convince you that things might get better, that things might change, that people might change. But the reality is *change* is a difficult process, and it's even more difficult when the person in question doesn't see a need for it.

If you're wondering if it is time to flee a toxic relationship, then strive to first understand the distinction between *hope* and *denial*. While *hope* can be constructive, *denial* is always destructive. We engage in denial when we refuse to acknowledge the reality of a situation. We ignore our partner's toxicity and attempt to rationalize the pain that they are inflicting upon us.

If you find yourself constantly justifying your partner's actions or playing defense for their behavior, then you may be caught in a cycle of denial, and it's time to reassess your relationship.

Question 2: Have your family or friends suggested that it's time to leave?

Conducting an objective analysis of your own relationship can be challenging, especially if your partner has been working behind the scenes to manipulate your perception of reality. Often, the only clear perspective to be had is from those who are outside looking in. If your friends or family have expressed concern about your relationship, or have asked if your partner is treating you well, then this might be an indicator that something is wrong, especially if multiple people have voiced such concerns independently.

Question 3: Are you being isolated? Or, have you found yourself self-isolating?

Toxic individuals often use *isolation* as a tactic to exert control over a submissive partner. If you're cut off from your support network, then your friends and family won't have an opportunity to provide you with an alternate perspective by which to gauge the health of your relationship. This tactic also makes it harder for you to leave because you may feel you have nowhere to go and no one to turn to for help. Alternatively, victims of abuse might also elect to *self-isolate*. They might actively avoid interacting with family or friends because they know that such encounters will only result in a critique of their situation or questions about their spouse's behavior.

In essence, isolation only serves to strengthen the toxic person's control over you while simultaneously weakening your ability to accurately evaluate your situation or your resolve to leave.

Question 4: Do you live in a state of fear?

Relationships are derived from love, not fear. If you find yourself constantly walking on eggshells around your partner—scared of saying or doing something that might upset him—then this may be a sign that the relationship is unhealthy. The victim of a toxic relationship might have many different types of fears.

- Do you fear that you might make a misstep that incites an emotional outburst?
- Do you fear that he will abandon you or isolate himself from all emotional interaction?
- Do you fear he will reach for a bottle?
- Do you fear that he will become physically violent?

A loving relationship cannot commence against a backdrop of fear. If you feel as if you're spending your days tiptoeing around a sleeping dragon, then it might be time for you to reevaluate the dynamics at play in your home and with your spouse.

Question 5: Have you lost your sense of self?

It is common for the victim of a toxic relationship to surrender her will to the demands of her partner. This submission might cause her to lose sight of her own identity, needs, and desires.

- Have you found that your decisions or actions are increasingly dictated by your partner?
- Have you neglected your personal interests, hobbies, or relationships—especially the ones that were so important to you in the past?
- Have you stopped expressing your opinion to reduce the possibility of rocking the boat in your relationship?
- Have you started to wonder if you're living for your partner's goals rather than your own?

If so, then you might be losing your sense of self.

It's crucial to understand that a healthy relationship should uplift and celebrate the uniqueness of both partners. If you can't recognize the person you've become in your current relationship, then it might be time to reevaluate your status and reclaim your individual autonomy.

Question 6: Have you exhausted all your other options?

It is common for couples to have disagreements and difficult periods. Keep in mind that your annoyances with your spouse are not necessarily the result of malevolence or pathological narcissism. Some relationships are indeed worth saving. If you and your partner have hit a rocky patch, then fleeing the relationship is not always the best course of action. It is common for couples to try things like:

- Having a friend or family member mediate a discussion about your marital woes.
- Allowing a window of opportunity in which trust can be rebuilt and sustained.
- Setting clear boundaries about crucial needs and concerns.
- Scheduling quality time together to get to know each other again.
- And seeking out professional counseling or therapy to help navigate through the issues and find constructive solutions.

Such steps can work. But, as we all know, they don't work for everyone. If you have exhausted all of your options, and your attempts to improve things have failed to bear fruit, then it might be time to reevaluate your relationship goals and consider whether or not the relationship is truly one worth sustaining.

Question 7: Is your partner abusive?

If your partner is engaging in physical or emotional abuse, then it's time to extract yourself from the situation. In this book, we have mentioned several forms of abuse—some are more subtle and more difficult to quantify than others. In general, you should make an effort to immediately flee a relationship in which your partner:

- Physically harms you in any way.
- Makes you fear for your safety if you were to leave.
- Threatens the physical safety of another person, like a child or someone else close to you.
- Confiscates your personal information, money, or ID cards in an effort to keep you contained.
- Consistently belittles, devalues, or shames you.
- Forces you into performing sexual acts or acts of physical abuse.

If you're unsure about your safety, seek out assistance from professionals or trustworthy family members. Reach out to local support groups, hotlines, or services that offer help and advice in such situations. Always remember that everyone deserves to feel safe, respected, and loved in a relationship. If that is not your experience, then it's time to reconsider taking the necessary steps to move on.

How to leave a toxic relationship

Unfortunately, leaving a toxic relationship can be a lot harder than getting into one. It might involve disentangling not just emotions, but also shared resources, living situations, and parental obligations. There's also the fear of the unknown, the potential for spousal revenge, and the grief of losing someone you most likely had a legitimate connection with. Regardless, it is essential to prioritize your mental, emotional, and physical wellbeing over that of a toxic partner. The process of leaving can be broken down into several steps to help make the transition smoother and safer. In this section, we will discuss these steps in detail, from establishing a support network to planning your exit strategy and rebuilding your life after a separation.

Step 1: Make sure your support network is ready first

Your exit from a toxic relationship should not be a solitary endeavor. It is crucial to have a support network that is aware of your situation and your intention to leave it. This could be family, friends, or professionals like therapists or counselors. Before you flee the nest, you must have some idea about where you are going to land. Additionally, in the days that follow your breakup, you will need strong people around you who can listen, provide advice, and practical support. Share your plans with a trusted individual and ensure they are prepared to offer emotional support and, if necessary, a safe place to stay. The more prepared your support network is, the easier it will be for you to summon the strength necessary to take the first critical leap out of your current toxic environment.

Step 2: Plan your exit

The degree to which you must plan your exit strategy is relative to the degree of your current entanglement. If you share a home, a car, or other financial assets with your partner, then things can get complicated. And, if you and your partner have children, then their welfare and safety will need to be attended to as well. Consult a professional if kids or property are involved in the mix, and be sure to understand all of your rights before making any brash decisions.

Step 3: Make your partner aware of your departure and your new boundaries

Your partner will find out about your departure in some fashion eventually. So, it might be best to enumerate the reasons for your retreat using clear and concise language. If having a conversation is no longer a viable option, consider writing a brief letter that explains your rationale for leaving and provides instructions regarding how communication is to commence in the future. This letter must not be a venue for blame or accusations. Instead, write in a straightforward manner and firmly declare your intention to terminate the relationship. Express your need for personal space and a time to heal in peace. And don't forget to keep a copy of the letter for your own records.

Step 4: Cut off contact with your partner

Extricating someone from your life used to be easier. A single woman could just get on a bus, move to a different city, and start her life anew. In fact, she might live out the rest of her days without hearing a single peep from her ex again. However, as many of us have experienced, ridding yourself of a persistently malevolent partner is tricky in the digital age.

The first avenue by which your ex will attempt to communicate is via cellphone. These days, ditching one's cellphone is not the easiest thing to do since our phones also function as a wallet, contact list, and bank account. Depending on the level of toxicity in your relationship, it might be worth it to go through the trouble of transferring all your data over to a new cellphone (with a new cellphone number). If you absolutely must talk to your ex (or his lawyer), you might consider using a "burner phone" for such conversations. That way, when the breakup has been finalized, you can simply ditch the burner phone and mitigate future communiqués from these parties.

The second avenue by which your ex will try to reinitiate contact is via social media—particularly Facebook, Instagram, and Snapchat. If you have a presence on any of these sites, you might want to consider deactivating your accounts or, in the least, blocking your ex from viewing your profile and messaging you. The persistent images and videos publicly displayed via social media have a way of amplifying the emotional stress of a breakup for both parties involved. So, it might be in your best interest to outright delete this content. You may also want to inform your mutual contacts about the situation so they can support you in maintaining your newly erected boundaries and protecting your privacy.

Step 5: Recover and rebuild
Leaving a toxic relationship can take a toll on your mental health. It's important to prioritize self-care during this time and to seek professional help if necessary. This might mean finding a therapist or counselor to talk through your feelings with, or it could mean setting aside time each day for activities that help you relax and rejuvenate. The process of healing can be a long and tender one, which is why we have devoted the entire next chapter to discussing this journey.

Ch. 9: How to recover from a toxic relationship

In 2022, the Oxford Dictionary selected "goblin mode" as their *Word of the Year*. They defined it as:

> ...a behavior which is unapologetically self-indulgent, lazy, slovenly, or greedy, typically in a way that rejects social norms or expectations.

In other words, when you go into *goblin mode*, you begin to act like a goblin. You sit in front of the TV watching Netflix and shoving pizza, Doritos, and beer down your throat. You set your cell phone to reject all incoming calls, and you wear pajamas everywhere you go.

I know that's what I did after every one of my relationships ended...

Following a breakup, it is normal to indulge in such comfort-seeking behaviors. And when you flee a *toxic* relationship, your willingness to abandon your health and hygiene may be compounded. Deciding to eat junk food and binge-watch TV shows is a way to seek refuge from your social obligations and cope with the stress of closing the door to one stage of your life. However, it is important to remember that, while these activities can provide temporary relief, you'll have to come out of goblin mode eventually, and return to the daily grind of self-improvement.

In this chapter, we'll explore several strategies for re-engaging with your daily life and rebuilding your confidence. This process involves mourning, acknowledging your emotions, reaching out for support when needed, and then, making a decision to continue along the path of self-discovery and self-actualization. Accepting the journey that lies before you can be a transformative experience, allowing you to heal, recover, learn from, and grow beyond the toxic relationship that has hindered your forward progress for so long.

Tip 1: Exercise

I admit it. I used to make fun of gym rats and fitness bros. Whenever I would read a pop psych article that prescribed "exercise" as a viable way to cure my angst, I'd immediately turn the page. But I was wrong.

The mind is part of the body. If you want to get your mind back in shape, you need to get your body in shape too. Exercise not only elevates your mood, it also helps regulate your sleep pattern and increase your energy levels, which are often disrupted following a traumatic life event. When you exercise, endorphins are released into your bloodstream. These natural *feel-good chemicals* (sometimes called the body's "natural painkillers") help to reduce stress and promote feelings of euphoria that help to counteract your depreciated mood.

If you're new to fitness, don't feel the need to join a gym or buy expensive equipment. Just start by doing some modest form of physical activity once a day, every day. A short jog around the block, a yoga routine, or a walk to the park, each of these excursions will contribute to the healing process. Get started on taking small, achievable steps that gradually build up your strength, resilience, and confidence. Try not to view your exercise sessions as a chore. Instead, consider them as an investment in yourself and your future happiness.

Tip 2: Eat healthy

Following my nastiest breakup, I did nothing but eat takeout food and sugary cereal for a month. Needless to say, I didn't feel great. The goblin food wasn't helping me move on. In fact, it was making things worse. Every time I would walk past the mirror, I would glance at my waistline and a flood of criticisms would pop into my head. Eventually, I realized that I couldn't live like this any longer. I decided to take charge of my refrigerator and make some changes to my eating habits. I started by eliminating junk food and incorporating more fruits, vegetables, lean proteins, and whole grains into my meals. I had to learn to see food as nourishment, not just as an analgesic designed to be taken during another *Game of Thrones* marathon.

Eventually, I developed a newfound appreciation for the power of good nutrition and how it directly impacted my physical health and mental health. I can't stress enough how much a balanced, healthy diet plays a vital role in maintaining mental wellness and aiding in the recovery process. So, make it a point to fuel your body with the nutrients it needs, and it will thank you in return.

Tip 3: Get some sleep

Depression and sleep problems often go hand in hand. If your aim is to get back on the ladder of self-improvement, then you need to monitor the duration, quality, and pattern of your sleep ritual.

- When it comes to your sleep **duration**, you should be getting around seven to nine hours of sleep each night. Depressed people often get too much or too little.
- When it comes to your sleep **quality**, know that there is a difference between the rejuvenating power of *deep sleep* and the kind of sleep we get when we collapse on the couch near a bottle of wine, with the TV blaring in the background, broadcasting the latest gadget from the *Home Shopping Network*.
- When it comes to your sleep **pattern**, it's best to get to bed at a reasonable time and plan on rising around eight hours later, not longer.

Recovering from a toxic relationship with a spouse often entails fleeing our primary residence and crashing in a guest bedroom, a hotel, or a room in a new apartment. During such escapades, the disruption of our sleep cycles is inevitable. Make efforts to try to counteract this by establishing a new sleep routine as soon as possible. Consider limiting screen time before bed, engaging in a relaxing activity like reading or meditating, and ensuring your sleeping environment is quiet, dark, and comfortable. Moreover, avoid consuming caffeine and alcohol close to bedtime as they can interfere with your sleep quality. If you still find it challenging to get to sleep, you might want to try natural remedies like chamomile tea or melatonin, though it's always best to consult with a healthcare professional before taking any new supplements.

Remember, sleep is a critical component of our physical and mental health. A well-rested mind is more resilient, allowing you to better cope with the emotional challenges that come with healing from a difficult relationship.

Tip 4: Stay connected with your support network

As we mentioned at the start of this chapter, it is natural to turn off your cell phone and retreat from your social circle following a breakup. This course of action is not always completely unwarranted because it is possible that *your* circle of friends is also *his* circle of friends. The person you fled may still be in contact with some of the people in your contact list. This can make social interactions difficult. As Bruno Mars sang in his 2012 breakup song "When I Was Your Man:"

When our friends talk about you, all it does is just tear me down,
'Cause my heart breaks a little when I hear your name.

I think we all know what it's like to hear someone utter the name of a former lover and then to become heartbroken all over again. However, despite the possibility of such perturbations, it is vital that you find a social outlet in which you can express your emotions and feel heard. Connection with others is crucial during periods of emotional distress; it helps us to remember that we are not alone in our struggle and that there are people who care about us and praying that we emerge from our shell a wiser person.

Tip 5: Don't stay connected via social media

When I expounded on the need to "stay connected," I wasn't referring to social media. As discussed in the previous chapter, the digital age provides us with a conduit by which we can zip into the lives of our former flings and experience the rollercoaster of emotions all over again. If you've recently ended a toxic relationship, the last thing you need to be looking at is their social media. Their curated life might look perfect regardless of how well they're actually doing. Their stunning selfies and subtle jabs will do you no good.

If the toxic person in your life is still connected to you via social media, then make an effort to cut ties. Depending on which social networks you share, the process of withdrawal might be difficult to accomplish. But try to unfriend and unfollow whoever you need to. And consider deleting your social media account entirely or perhaps starting a new one.

Tip 6: Keep your mind engaged

If your toxic relationship has prompted you to relocate and start over again in a new city, then you have to cope with the dual problem of nurturing a new social circle as well as a new set of daily activities, possibly even a new career. It is natural to feel intimidated by such challenges, which is why so many people turn inward and let their minds dwell on past experiences or future worries. While it's important to give your emotions time to process, spending too much time ruminating over past events can hamper your healing process and prevent you from reengaging with life. To counteract this, make an active effort to keep your mind stimulated with some sort of daily activity. We already mentioned exercise. But don't be afraid to delve into social hobbies like:

- Joining a social book club or cooking class,
- Participating in community events,
- Taking up hobbies such as painting, gardening, or playing a musical instrument,
- Outdoor activities like hiking and sightseeing,
- Or volunteer work.

By focusing your cognitive faculties on learning or personal growth, you not only occupy your mind with constructive thoughts, but you also improve your self-confidence and open yourself up to new experiences and new social opportunities. The positive feedback you receive from such undertakings can help shift your perspective and aid in your emotional recovery.

Tip 7: Develop a healthy relationship with your inner critic

The army drill sergeant doesn't scream at his new recruits because he's trying to humiliate them for the sheer joy of it. Instead, the drill sergeant screams at his recruits because he wants to instill in them the discipline and resilience needed to stay alive should they ever be called upon to face a real threat.

Of course, we are all born with a drill sergeant in our heads. He's the guy who owns that little voice that makes a comment whenever you eat a pastry, cheat on your taxes, pour that third glass of wine, or walk by a mirror. Our drill sergeant can be a demanding one. And sometimes, his critiques are uncalled for. But just know that he means well. More specifically, he's trying to keep you alive the best way he knows how. The voice of censure that emanates from the bowels of your brain (your ego) was tuned via millions of years of evolution. It knows a lot about you. It's been with you for your entire life. And its only job is to keep you alive and multiplying. Your emotions are the tools by which it attempts to prod you to action. But emotion is a broad sword. And sometimes, your ego flings it about too wildly.

Enlightenment comes when we learn to accept the critique offered by the drill sergeant in our head as just one of many possible bits of advice. His warnings are designed to prevent us from engaging in an activity that might result in a physically or socially undesirable outcome. He'll say things like:

- "I don't think you're prepared to give this presentation."
- "I don't think you're good enough to do this."
- "I don't think they'll respond well to your offer."
- "I don't think you'll ever recover from this."

If such ruminations remain unchecked, you may never be able to progress beyond your current state in life and continue your walk down the path of self-actualization. To manage such intrusive thoughts, we must learn to recognize when the voice in your head is offering useful advice, and when he's merely spouting baseless fears. That's the hard part.

When you hear this voice, pause and consider whether the critique is valid or merely an expression of fear or self-doubt. Take a moment to ponder the reality of the negative assertions and counteract them with positive affirmations or evidence of your past successes. In this manner, your inner critic can be a fruitful asset. Able to act as a partially functioning (but still useful) compass. A guide that will usually point you in the correct general direction, but who should not be relied on for everything, and should not be allowed to dictate your self-worth and happiness.

Remember, your inner critic is part of you, but it does not define you. Treat him like a stern football coach, not an infallible demigod. Developing a healthier relationship with your inner critic is not about silencing it but about learning to augment its input in a way that supports your personal growth.

Tip 8: Pursue what you want out of life

When you're in the grip of a toxic relationship, it is common to abandon your own goals in order to pursue the goals of your significant other. But when you finally flee this relationship, you may find that you have lost touch with your own ambitions and dreams. It might feel like you're sitting atop an unmanned craft, set adrift in a sea of uncertainty. We all lose our bearings every once in a while. But this need not be cause for alarm. Instead, see this time in your life as an opportunity to reevaluate your goals and reorient yourself toward the things that truly matter.

If you still don't know what you truly value yet, it can sometimes be helpful to divide your goals into multiple categories. These categories might include:

- health and fitness
- career
- family
- friends
- romance
- finances
- hobbies
- travel

- life skills
- spirituality

This is by no means an exhaustive list. And you shouldn't feel the immediate need to set goals in all of these areas. Start small. Picking two or three items to concentrate your efforts on, and then make a decision to better your life in these domains.

Whether it's pursuing a long-ignored passion, embarking on a new career, or simply reclaiming your sense of self, remember that you are the author of your own story. And this is your chance to write a chapter that reflects the authentic you, not a character that has been edited to suit someone else's narrative.

Tip 9: Focus on the present, not the past

People who have fled a particularly distressing experience sometimes develop *Post Traumatic Stress Disorder* (PTSD). Symptoms of this mental condition can vary from person to person. But they typically come in the form of:

- **Intrusive Memories**: Such as recurrent memories of the traumatic event, flashbacks, or nightmares.
- **Avoidance Behaviors**: Such as evading people, places, or things that remind you of the event or the parties involved.
- **Negative Changes in Thinking and Mood**: Such as persistent negative feelings about oneself or difficulties starting new relationships.
- **Increased Sensitivity to Stimuli**: Such as being easily startled or frightened by loud noises. Subjects may also have trouble sleeping, trouble concentrating, or may be prone to angry outbursts or aggression.

If you think you might be suffering from PTSD, then seek out professional counseling. Resources are widely available, from community mental health centers to specialized trauma therapists. Professionals can provide you with an appropriate therapeutic approach to guide you toward recovery and healing.

However, not everyone who goes through a bad breakup should seek out a diagnosis of PTSD. Ending *any* relationship can be a stressful and emotional experience—even if the dissolution was on good terms. Feelings of sadness and confusion are common. And people may be haunted by the memories of past interactions or horrified by the loss of what could have been.

Have you ever lain awake all night, replaying the same memory again and again?

- Maybe it was about the last argument you had with your spouse.
- Maybe it was about the first night you met, or the first night you kissed.
- Maybe it was about the moment when you realized your relationship was beyond repair.

Such ruminations are common following a breakup. But it's important to prevent the midnight movies playing in your head from halting your forward progress.

Many people on this planet live in the past. They immerse their mind in a sea of "what-ifs" and "could-have-beens." They become mired in memories and regrets, intent on mentally reliving a lost period of their life, while shunning any opportunities for new experiences that might present themselves in the here and now. This attitude, while understandable in the throes of heartbreak, can stunt emotional growth and prolong the healing process. As Epicurus wrote:

> **Do not spoil what you have by desiring what you have not; remember that what you now have was once among the things you only hoped for.**

While the past may have shaped you, it does not fully define you. Each moment is a new chance to grow, learn, and progress along the path before you. You must view your past missteps as learning experiences, not as irreversible blunders. Insisting on dwelling on the past is like trying to drive a car while looking in the rear-view mirror. The rear-view mirror has an important function—that's why they put them in every car. But, most of the time, if you want to move forward, it's best to keep your eyes on the road ahead.

Conclusion

Throughout this book, I have attempted to provide some advice about how you might go about dealing with the bullies, narcissists, liars, and manipulators that have stumbled across your path. Navigating the complex labyrinth of their veiled intentions requires understanding and patience. I hope that the strategies we've outlined have equipped you with the tools you need to get started countering their toxicity. Managing the multitudinous idiosyncrasies of our friends and family can be a challenging endeavor, even in the best of times. But if the fates insist on sending bullies and narcissists to obstruct our path, then our skill in traversing such multifaceted obstacles will be put to the test. I don't have to remind you of how taxing and draining such encounters can be.

Relationships are hard. Toxic relationships are even harder. But the most difficult relationship you'll ever manage is the one you have with yourself.

So, be kind to yourself.

Take some time for yourself.

Take some time to think.

Socrates wrote that "The unexamined life is not worth living." If you're still healing from a relationship gone bad, don't be afraid to seek out a professional counselor to talk to. At the least, be sure to set aside thirty minutes each day for quiet self-reflection. You might call this period your time for rumination, introspection, contemplation, or meditation. Regardless of your label for this time block, ensure that it is not open-ended. To avoid getting lost in thought, get in the habit of doing something productive as soon as the thirty minutes are up.

Remember, our progress down the path of enlightenment is achieved by *walking*, not by *sulking*. We should opt for *action* over *naval gazing* whenever the choice presents itself. This means embracing the purposeful action steps that are required to thrive and prosper, as well as accepting the everyday malaise of the human experience. As the Buddhist monks would say:

After enlightenment, the laundry.

Developing an intuitive understanding of the grand clockwork that spins between your ears is a lifelong pursuit. The ancient Greeks espoused the value of engaging in this venture with the aphorism *"temet nosce"* or "know thyself." It is one of the three maxims inscribed in the pronaos of the temple at Delphi. Like so many artifacts of antiquity, we can only guess at the original intent of its author. Plato said to "know thyself" means to understand one's own character and behaviors deeply; to develop an awareness of both our virtues and our vices, our strengths and our weaknesses, our hopes and our fears. This awareness is essential to achieving personal growth and inner fulfillment. For it is only after you truly know *yourself* that no one else will ever be able to dictate who you are (i.e., no one will ever be able to bully you again).

Of course, in order to truly know ourselves, we must first acquire a large repertoire of reference experiences. We meet new people. We fall in love. We fall out of love. We journey to distant lands. We stumble. We stand back up. We press on. And then we do it all over again. At each step of the way, your subconscious mind absorbs these experiences and calibrates itself to better understand the world and your place in it. It analyzes the lessons learned from your *triumphs* as well as your *failures*. It learns to navigate life's rocky terrain based on the feedback provided by your *heroes* as well as your *villains*.

Since you purchased this book, you probably have one or two villains on your mind. And you've probably allowed their toxicity to seep into your life. Their presence might be hampering your goals, hindering your dreams, clouding your perspective, and disrupting your inner peace. We have spent the last several chapters discussing some strategies to manage their mayhem. Yet, when the toxicity in such relationships becomes too overwhelming, it may be in your interest to elect for self-preservation over confrontation. Retreat, accept, and forgive. These might feel like concessions. But such a strategy can also be an act of courage and self-love.

Seizing the reins of your life back from a malevolent driver is often the only rational thing to do. And yet, in doing so, we can't help but feel a sense of guilt or failure. We regret our inability to remedy a doomed relationship, even after we know that the person we once held so dear is not who we believed them to be. In such a scenario, we must strive to remain cognizant of our own limitations. Our ability to positively influence our own life outcome is limited. Even more limited is our ability to affect the life outcomes of those around us.

In *The Art of Living*, the Greek philosopher Epictetus (c. 50-135 AD) wrote:

Happiness and freedom begin with a clear understanding of one principle: Some things are within our control, and some things are not. It is only after you have faced up to this fundamental rule and learned to distinguish between what you can and cannot control that inner tranquility and outer effectiveness become possible.

The American theologian Reinhold Niebuhr echoed similar sentiments in his famous "Serenity Prayer," written in 1943. It reads:

God, grant me the serenity to accept the things I cannot change, courage to change the things I can, and wisdom to know the difference.

Each of us feels an innate desire to help the people we love. We secretly harbor notions of rectifying wrongs and rebuilding the foundations of relationships that have crumbled long ago. However, while the instinct to help and to mend is commendable, we must understand that psychological stagnation and immutability are the default states of man. Most people do not respond well to disruptions of their psyche, assaults on their ego, or critiques of their mode of living. The urge to maintain the status quo often prevails over any prospect of an avenue for personal growth. Even as we reach out to help others, they might be more likely to *retreat* from our hand than to grasp it. Some situations cannot be fixed. Some relationships cannot be salvaged. Instead:

- *Acceptance* might be all we can provide to those who lack the capacity to change.
- *Retreat* might be our best strategy if we are to preserve our mental health and wellbeing.
- *Forgiveness* may be the only gift we can give to those who have wronged us—even if they don't deserve it.

Relieving ourselves of the burden of anger and resentment is a pivotal step on the road to attaining inner peace. Instead of spending one more moment entangled in the energy-draining torrent of conflict and consternation, we have the prerogative to adopt a stoic stance when confronting our woes.

- We must be free to rid ourselves of the desire to affect every immovable object in our universe.
- We must be free to seek out someone to love bravely, even if we risk heartbreak in our pursuit.
- We must be free to forgive.

This peace offering need not be wholly altruistic. As Johnathan Lockwood Huie wrote:

Forgive others, not because they deserve forgiveness, but because you deserve peace.

Did you like the book?

Thank you for coming along for the ride with me. I really hope you enjoyed the book. If so, then please consider writing a book review. For an independent author like me, book reviews mean *everything*, and I personally read each one.

Or, if you have any suggestions on how I can improve my next book, don't be shy about contacting me. I look forward to hearing from you!

Thanks again,

Serena

Made in the USA
Columbia, SC
01 July 2025